What early readers want
As If We Were

D0356367

"Are you almost ready to throw up y
itics and citizenship? Before you do, please read this book. It will
change your idea about what's possible in America, and very likely stir you to action to make it happen—as if you were a grownup,
taking charge of your own future."

THOM HARTMANN, author of *We the People,*
***A Return to Democracy,* and** *The Last Hours of Ancient Sunlight*

★ ★ ★ ★ ★

"This potent book comes along at one of the most critical times in
American history. If you care about our future, our politics, the
soul of this country, you'll know exactly what I mean before you've
finished three pages."

JEAN HOUSTON, Ph.D, author of *Jump Time* **and** *The Possible Human,*
Director of International Programs in Social Artistry

★ ★ ★ ★ ★

"This is breakthrough thinking, simple and daring at the same time.
You don't need to agree with every word to realize that Jeff Golden
has captured the voice and the spirit that could renew American
politics. Buy two, and give one to a friend who's given up on public life. Better yet, send one to a politician who wants to remember
why they got into the business in the first place."

MATT MILLER, *Fortune Magazine* **columnist and author of**
The Two Percent Solution: Fixing America's Problems
in Ways Liberals and Conservatives Can Love

★ ★ ★ ★ ★

"They say politics is the art of the possible. As a practitioner, student
and teacher of politics for most of my life, I have run up against the
limits of that art more times than I can remember. The wonder of
these pages is that they push outward the limits of what's possible
in a fresh and fascinating way. *As If We Were Grownups* is a fine,
important book."

BARBARA ROBERTS, former Governor of Oregon,
political science professor at Harvard's Kennedy School
of Government and Portland State University

"Am I glad I found this book. It restored my sometimes-wavering faith that common sense, human connection and a bit of reflection about what's genuinely in our self-interest can overcome short-sighted dogma and the social carnage of big-money politics. What an overdue, bracing and realistic dose of hope."

**NEALE DONALD WALSCH, international speaker
and author of the *Conversations with God* series**

★ ★ ★ ★ ★

"I'm delighted to find in these pages a prescription that could stanch the hemorrhage of public confidence. This book helps pave the way to a new national political ethic."

LES AUCOIN, nine-term U.S. Congressman, Oregon's First District

★ ★ ★ ★ ★

"Jeff Golden honors Americans in treating us as if we were grownups. One vote cast here for a good thinker, a fine speech-writer, and a real grownup."

**RICHARD D. HEFFNER, founding director of WNET-TV and
longtime host of public television's *The Open Mind***

★ ★ ★ ★ ★

"Jeff Golden's *As If We Were Grownups* is long overdue. He has hit upon a compelling political alchemy for our times: one part prag-matism, one part idealism, one small but crucial part humor."

Political Science Professor BILL HUGHES, Southern Oregon University

★ ★ ★ ★ ★

"Democracy, as is often said, is a participatory sport. It doesn't work unless we're all thinking about the consequences of the actions our elected representatives take. They're the hired help, which means we have a very direct role to play in who they are and what they do. *As If We Were Grownups*, Jeff Golden's collection of 'suicidal' speech-es is a solid contribution to the education of voters, leaders, and opinion-makers. Its provocative arguments and persuasive yet respectful tone will add measurably to the thinking person's ability to sort through some of the most important issues of our day—and then help choose the hired help."

**BRAD KNICKERBOCKER, Senior Staff Writer,
*The Christian Science Monitor***

As If We Were Grownups

★ ★ ★ ★ ★

Other books by Jeff Golden

Watermelon Summer
Lippincott and Company, New York

Forest Blood
www.forestblood.com

AS IF WE WERE GROWNUPS

A Collection of "Suicidal"
Political Speeches That Aren't

★ JEFF GOLDEN ★

RiverWood Books

This book is dedicated to the Third Generation.

★ ★ ★ ★ ★

"It does not matter so much where we are . . . as the direction in which we are moving."

JOHANN VON GOETHE

Table of Contents

Introduction

From One
Who's Been There

★ ★ ★ ★ ★

My life has been spent in politics: four years in the Oregon Legislature, eighteen years in the United States Congress, a decade as an analyst and teacher of political science. Over the course of those years it has been harder than I can describe to watch the hemorrhage of public confidence in America's modern political institutions and the officials who inhabit them. I'm delighted to find in these pages a prescription that could stanch the bleeding. Here's a compelling case for politicians of all stripes to stop selling cotton candy — giving it away, really — and to start trusting that we voters are adults who can cope with what we need to hear, unpleasant or unsettling as it might sometimes be.

Jeff Golden shrewdly doesn't call on us to deny our self interest. Instead these chapters, as he puts it, challenge "the way modern politics has us *calculating* our self-interest." The result is a compendium of speeches for candidates ready to confront what professional handlers would call some of the most dangerous issues in U.S. politics. Together the speeches illustrate how a candidate might stir the electorate out of a torpor induced by a political class determined to avoid what might shake voter sensibilities, thus skirting the nation's fundamental problems. Golden makes a powerful case that such tough love can inspire broad support among voters, who intuitively know that all too often they are being served baby food. He suggests that when voters know they are being used, they ironically hold politicians in low regard even as candidates pander to them.

As I read these pages my mind returned to a conversation I had with a colleague on the floor of the U.S. House of Representatives in the 1970s. Before us was a vote on a modest gasoline tax. My colleague had decided — against his better judgment — to oppose the tax. "You and the others are right that the tax is needed," he said. "But I just can't sell it to my district. To tell you the truth, I don't have the energy to try." So he gave his voters what he thought they wanted: lower gasoline prices. Over the length of the congressional session, this became a trait of his. But if my friend thought that constant appeasement of his constituents would create for him a long career in Washington, he was badly mistaken. His constituents soundly rejected him in his third bid for reelection.

In my own case, the U.S. government's decision to grant citizenship to South Vietnamese boat people in the mid-Seventies was highly controversial in my district. In town meetings back home, I heard a chorus of objections to "letting more foreigners into our country to take our jobs and use taxpayer provided public welfare services." I disagreed and pulled no punches with my audiences. "First," I said, "We are dealing with people who believed in America during the war. Secondly, they fled because their assistance to our nation would mark them and their families for death. And third, thousands of these same individuals are bobbing in makeshift boats in the South China Sea, often victimized by Thai pirates who steal what few possessions they carry with them and force fathers and brothers to watch sexual assaults on their wives and sisters. You may disagree with me, but if the Statue of Liberty means anything, Americans have a moral obligation to welcome these Vietnamese to our shores." I was sailing against the wind, going against the grain. But the auditorium broke into applause and the objections ended there.

This is exactly the approach laid out in these pages. This book helps pave the way to a new national political ethic. Golden's persuasive case is that Americans want adult treatment, perhaps even more than agreement, from their leaders.

The author draws a bead on the power of special interest campaign money. In his proposed speech advocating full public financing of campaigns (considered a potato way too hot to handle in the "real" world), he shows an astute understanding of how the escalation of such money corrupts modern American politics. It is not that sacks of money are deposited on politicians' desks with voting instructions, he writes. It isn't that a donor very often comes back around later and says, "I helped you; now you help me." It's subtler and more suffocating than that, Golden suggests. Says he:

"Instead of [bag drops] what we have in today's politics is a very powerful question. It is almost never asked out loud — it doesn't have to be — but it runs through the thinking of almost everyone who holds an elective office that takes a lot of money to win, and it shines brightest at the moment that a high-stakes decision must be made. The question is: *What will my big contributors think about this?"*

This book lights the way for politicians. Its larger and more critical audience is the rest of us — the consumers of politics — whose self-interest is best served by being told fundamental facts, not fiction or *non sequiturs,* and by being served arguments that reach, as Lincoln said, "the better angels of our nature." It is a politics that we can still have — if we demand it.

LES AUCOIN
United States Congressman
from Oregon's First District, 1974–1992

★ ★ ★ ★ ★

★ I ★

Forewords

Where We Begin

First Words:
We Can Do Better Than This

★ ★ ★ ★ ★

Seconds Words:
**Our Cycle of Politics:
Spoiling Spoiled Children**

★ ★ ★ ★ ★

"In rivers and bad governments,
the lightest things
swim at the top."

BENJAMIN FRANKLIN

First Words

We Can Do Better Than This

You're about to read speeches we desperately need to hear from candidates who want to hold high office. Will we hear them soon, say in the next national campaign? Right now the odds aren't good. But you can make them better.

Don't just read these speeches. Photocopy them, scan them into your computer and email them, rip them straight out of the book. Then send them to candidates that you might vote for. You have my permission. You have my plea.

Tell your candidates exactly why you're sending these speeches to them: not so they'll agree with every opinion (*you're* not going to agree with every opinion you read here, friend), but so that they'll know that shuck and jive won't work anymore. Tell them that for the sake of everything they say they want for America, it's time to ignore their certified-smart consultants and start dealing with us as if we were grownups.

Tell them, as soon as you finish this book, that you're ready.

Second Words
Our Cycle of Politics:
Spoiling Spoiled Children

I'm going to guess that you don't respect the quality of contemporary American politics. You're wondering how I know that, right? It could be highly-attuned psychic powers, or it could be that there's almost nobody left in America who respects the quality of contemporary politics. The way people frame their disdain, the images and words they use, differ widely across economic class and educational status. But the core opinion about the quality of our politics is shared about as widely as an opinion can be.

I'll guess further that you've said or at least thought one or more of these things about the people at the top of the political heap:

"They don't care about a damn thing except getting
   re-elected."
"Know how you can tell when politicians are lying?
   They move their lips."
"They're completely spineless."
"They just say what they think we want to hear."
"Why aren't there any real leaders anymore?"
"They talk to us like we're children."

And while we're all talking and nodding and appreciating each other's cleverness, politicians and political consultants are having their own conversations. They are talking, more quietly and discretely than we talk, about us. Some of what they say, or at least think, is

"You have talk to them like children."
"They can hold exactly one thought in their minds at a
time. Two, *maybe*, on a good day."
"They say they want honesty. They don't want honesty. They
want candy-canes and chocolate sundaes and big cars and
a fancy house and someone else to send the bill to."
"They wouldn't know leadership if it smacked them
in the face."
"Mencken had it right: 'Nobody ever went broke
underestimating the American public'."

These are the lyrics of the politics that we've created. It is a co-creation, actually, between those who relentlessly seek our vote, those of us who give it to them, and those so disgusted they've stopped voting for anyone, often with the peculiar notion that they thereby shed any responsibility for this mess.

This mess takes the shape of a cycle. The political class, amplified by news media that doesn't like complexity, talks to us like children so forcefully and repetitively that we become political children. Not "children" as in pure, uninhibited, innocent, playful and trusting. Rather "children" as in immature, undiscerning, self-absorbed, grabby, uncaring about the impact our gain has on others, ignorant or unmindful that life has trade-offs in general and that there's a social contract in particular that gives us benefits in return for personal limitations — children, to distill it down to the core trait that drives modern political strategy, that get angry and spiteful when they hear what they don't want to hear. What *we* don't want to hear.

Then as undiscerning children with no sense of trade-offs, we gravitate in the largest numbers to aspiring leaders who tell us what we want to hear. We want to hear that we are great children who make our country great. We want to hear that we can have more benefits for less cost tomorrow, and still more for less the next day. If there are any hurdles in the way, we want to hear they're the work of some dark Other, not the consequence of anything we've done, so that they can be removed without much pain or bother to us. And we don't want to hear a whole lot of details about any of it, because we want to go out and play.

This doesn't sound exactly like you, does it? It's not exactly like anyone I know. Very few people purely fit this type. Yet it seems to be one of the temperamental currents that run through almost all of us. And beyond individual personalities, there's a kind of gravitational field that sets in. The political media drumbeat tells us again and again that we can have what we want without costs or consequences, if we'll just embrace and believe in the Greatness That Is America. Something in us gets pulled: the spooked-child part that just wants Daddy to take care of it, the conflict-averse part that doesn't want to interrupt the flow, maybe the conforming part that doesn't want to be pegged as "negative" when everyone else seems to be rallying to the cheerful call.

Whatever the psychological under-story, enough of us are pulled far enough to create a clear empirical pattern: when other key elements are roughly equal, we consistently elect the candidate who tells us what children would most want to hear.

The media calls these candidates "upbeat." We like upbeat.

And the consultants who crafted the campaign messages for spoiled children take a bow, a hefty paycheck and maybe a Caribbean vacation before moving on to the next campaign with their proven wisdom. "Tell me," their next client asks, "what do you think it was that won your last campaign?"...

★ ★ ★ ★ ★

This self-confirming cycle is a self-inflicted wound to our body politic. When we craft our politics for spoiled children we end up with the accumulated mountain of consequences that those children didn't want to hear about, much less address. This is the bare naked core of unsustainability. It can't go on.

This book is about breaking the cycle. As with most powerful cycles, you can spend a lot of time looking for a loose seam to start unwinding it, arguing about what's cause and what's effect. A moment comes when you just have to pick a place and go at it.

I pick campaign speeches. What if a presidential or other top-level candidate consciously decided to break the cycle? What if s/he consistently talked to us as if we were grownups?

Some popular books and films have skirted close to this premise. With the film *Bulworth* Warren Beatty bet that the spectacle of a U.S. Senator speaking his true unedited thoughts on touchy social issues would strike us as so absurd that we'd laugh. We did. Jerzy Kozinski told an even more elemental story in *Being There*. What happens when Chauncey Gardiner, who innocently tells his untainted truth with such luminescent simplicity, drops into the world of politics? We passionately welcome him as the authentic hero we have been waiting for.

This book isn't about Chauncey Gardiner. *Being There* is a lovely fable and *Bulworth* is a delicious satire, but for their heroes to thrive in politics, we Americans would have to change more than we're going to.

Those stories can work in worlds that we like to imagine. This book aims to work in the world we have. The speeches you're about to read would have to be delivered in a country of real people, frightened, wary and weary people who get their information from media corporations that don't hold informing the citizenry as their primary goal. All that magically melts away in the movies. It doesn't out here. If these speeches don't speak powerfully to our sense of self-interest, then they're about as valuable as chunks of *Bulworth* script, except less funny.

Self-interest is the fuel of politics. We are invariably going to vote our own self-interest, to use the historic phrase, as God gives us light to see it. That's fine. More than fine, that is exactly what we're supposed to do in our role as citizens, and we always do it. No book could or should change that. These speeches mean to challenge instead the way modern politics has us *calculating* our self-interest. This book asserts that we'll serve our own interests better with a grownup's perspective. Since political campaigns have mightily obscured that point over the years, this book looks to politicians to nudge us back to a self-interest-based politics that actually serves our interests.

Seasoned political consultants (reading this, no doubt, on a Caribbean beach after recent wins) might agree completely that modern politics is a childish self-reinforcing cycle. But they would probably scoff at the suggestion that a high-level candidate could do much to break it. What if a focused committed politician ignored the expensive advice and decided to find out? What if s/he set out to prove you can actually *thrive* in politics by talking to voters like grownups? What would s/he be saying?

This introduction could go on as most do, with lots of suggestions about how to think about the book that follows. You don't need that. You're grownups.

★ II ★

Spoken Words

The Speeches

★ ★ ★ ★ ★

★ ★ ★ ★ ★

*"Man is by nature a
political animal."*

ARISTOTLE, *Politics*

One

You Should Pay for My Campaign

Telling a National Shriners Meeting
It's Time for Public Campaign Financing

It's a true privilege to have the chance to talk to you this evening. I'm privileged to stand in this large hall with every seat filled by people who want to hear what I have to say — or at least you've done a fine job putting attentive expressions on your faces. And the truth is that, for someone running for higher office, it's even a bigger privilege to have those big-lensed video cameras pointed at me, and to see those microphones and laptops among the press corps out there.

I use the word "privilege" not as a pleasant throw-away that we candidates feel obliged to use at the beginning of speeches to show our modesty. I use the word precisely. I have the privilege of being one of the very few, quote, **serious candidates**, end quote, in this race, and that's why this hall is full. And tomorrow I'm likely to be a slightly more quote, **serious**, end quote, candidate, because the clips of the video these good people are shooting will appear on network news shows, and some of the material getting tap-tapped into those laptops will show up in stories that a lot of people will read tomorrow morning. As one of the very few **serious candidates**, I am one of the very few people who can be elected president this year.

What makes me "serious," other than the fact that the jokes I slip into my talks aren't very funny? There are a few reasons. I could talk to you about the powerful message of this campaign, how deeply it resonates with Americans, about the relentless dedication of our staff, about how well my resume fits the job I'm applying for. In other words, I could give you the same speech every other candidate will give you. But let's put that off to another day. Today let's talk about the one element required for anyone, no matter how good or bad his or her ideas, programs, characters and intentions, to be a **serious candidate**.

It's money. Lots and lots of money. Whether I have something good to offer America or not, I would never be standing here, with all of *you* sitting there, without a lot of money. It happens that I'm proud of the way we've raised money, with a huge number of donations small enough to keep supporters from even imagining they have special say in the decisions I'd make as President. But that doesn't change the defining fact of American politics at this level: you don't get let in to play without a twenty or thirty million dollar ticket, and the ante is going up all the time.

And all of us know it. If there's a single opinion on politics that almost every breathing American shares, this has to be it. We don't all *voice* this opinion in the same way; it has a different sound depending on who you're talking to. Ask someone from an organization like Common Cause and you'll get a description of the elaborate plumbing system that moves cash around Washington, complete with statistical graphics on the correlation between campaign contributions and legislative votes. Ask the driver of the next cab you climb into and she may just say, "Well, yeah, of course, they're all a bunch of crooks. They're just there to line their own pockets. What, this is news to you?" Americans of all ages, educations, incomes, parties and outlooks simply know that high-level politics is disfigured by special interest money. If there's a belief about American politics that more people share, someone will have to tell me what it is.

What's striking in the face of this unified American opinion is how huffy and offended politicians can get when they hear it. *The very idea, they will tell you, that my vote is for sale is so ludicrous that it doesn't deserve a response.* Some of them may be speaking from genuine outrage. For others, it's a time-tested maneuver: take a critic's charge and exaggerate it to a size that seems too extreme or absolute to believe. *Anyone donating to my campaign knows full well they can't buy me. All they're buying is good government* — and maybe, as the more candid sometimes admit, future access: *They know I'll listen to what they have to say.*

Ladies and gentleman, let's be clear about what vote-buying does and doesn't look like in American politics today. Big contributors don't haul canvas sacks of money with black dollar signs printed on the side into the offices of politicians, plop the bags down on the desk, twirl their mustaches, blow cigar smoke in our faces and give us marching orders. That isn't necessary.

Instead of canvas sacks and cigars, what we have in today's politics is a very powerful question. It is almost never asked out loud — it doesn't have to be — but it runs through the thinking of almost everyone who holds an elective office that takes a lot of money to win, and it shines brightest at the moment that a high-stakes decision must be made. The question . . . is . . .

"What will my big contributors think about this?"

This question is so deeply woven into the fabric of our politics that it's often not conscious. Some legislators might not even think that they're asking it. They are, and they'll keep asking it as long as political survival depends on preserving the good will and open checkbooks of a few special supporters. And we have to expect some of that; it might even be a reasonable question somewhere in the course of a long complex deliberation. But when the impact on campaign contributors is the first or second question that comes to mind instead of the ninth or tenth, we can't pretend that our system puts the public interest first. It puts identifiable *special* interests first, interests that may or may not have much overlap with the public interest.

How do we separate healthy political activism from bribery in campaign contributions? How do we exclude, or at least make less powerful, the money that expects a return beyond good, honest, public-interested government? That's what the campaign finance reform movement has been about for decades now. It has focused mostly on limiting the amounts of money or services or resources that various people or organizations or coalitions can give to various candidates or parties or committees. None of these efforts have worked very well.

Some of the early straightforward versions were overturned by the courts as violations of the contributors' freedom of political expression. Later attempts to thread that needle of First Amendment rights have sacrificed logic and common-sense to legal strategies, so that we're left with measures so complex that their creators have trouble understanding them, with consequences and contradictions no one intended. You don't have to look any further than the famous McCain-Feingold Act to see that. In the lore of contemporary news coverage McCain-Feingold was a rare and dramatic triumph of good government over corruption. In fact it was a well-intentioned reform that was sliced, diced and pasteurized by legal and political strategies into an snarled jumble of rules and restrictions that may be causing more problems than it solved.

I believe that's bound to happen with reform efforts that depend on limiting donations. Minds that are capable of designing intricate regulatory systems like McCain-Feingold are plenty capable of designing ways around them. In ways well-known and ways mysterious, money seeps. Like water on an old and brittle flat roof, it will find its way inside.

I believe there's a better way. Tell me what you think of this idea: I think *you* should pay for my campaign. That's right. I believe some of the hard-earned dollars you pay to the government in taxes should go towards *my* campaign to get elected. I suppose I should add that some should also go to my opponents in this race, and to all the *bona fide* candidates — and I'll define that in a moment — running for national offices. Tax dollars partially support some presidential campaigns today, but I'm talking about much more than that.

What I'm talking about is called public campaign financing. Whenever it comes up in the form of a specific proposal, we also call it something else: "dead on arrival." That's not hard to understand. In fact, I can't think of an easier job than writing the television spots *against* public financing that would flood the airwaves. You'd start with a pleasant-looking older couple sipping coffee and reading the newspaper at their breakfast nook, with a bouquet of fresh daisies on the table and soft sunshine pouring through the window, maybe some easy-listening music in the background. The peaceful moment is shattered when the man slams the paper down, his face turning red and angry. "Okay," he says, "that's it! That is IT!"

"What is it, Bob?" she'll say.

"Do you know what these guys are trying to do now?" he says.

"What guys, honey?" she says.

"These *crooks!* These politicians! They're tired of raising money to get elected, so now they're just going to take *our* money and put it in their campaigns!"

"Oh, now, honey, calm down." she says. "You know that can't be right. The papers are always getting it wrong these days."

As she reaches over to pat his arm, bring in a deep baritone announcer's voice: BUT THEY'RE NOT GETTING IT WRONG. IT'S REALLY TRUE. IF SOME POLITICIANS GET THEIR WAY, YOU'LL SOON BE PAYING FOR *THEIR* CAMPAIGNS TO GET ELECTED— FOR THEIR BUMPER STICKERS AND BUTTONS, THEIR ADVERTISING AND THEIR FIRST-CLASS PLANE TICKETS — EVEN IF YOU DISAGREE WITH EVERY-THING THEY STAND FOR!

Well, stop right there! Who needs a system like that?

We do. If I'm the only candidate in this race saying so, it's not because I'm the only one who believes it. It's because others don't think voters will pay enough attention to understand the argument for it. I don't know if they're right about that or not. I do know that this is too important to gloss over.

What we're talking about right now — the way campaigns for high office are paid for in America— is the *fulcrum* of our ability to improve our national life. If we can't get it right then we can't expect the big public decisions to be made on the basis of what's best for most Americans, and all of our passionate debates on the merits of issues like taxation, national defense, education, property rights, business and the environment, health care, *all* of it . . . is a waste of breath.

I call that important enough to deserve an honest and care-ful conversation about public financing. And what I don't think is honest — or at least what gets the discussion off-track at the beginning — is the notion that the only people benefitting from the dollars needed to get out candidates' messages are the can-didates themselves. Listen again to the angry man in my sample TV ad: "They're just going to take *our* money and put it in their campaigns!"

We have to challenge that notion. If we still believe that "representative government" is more than a phrase in high school textbooks, we have to insist that these campaigns are not for the candidates, *but for us.* If we forget that, the opponents of public financing have an argument that can't be beat. One of the most articulate of those opponents is Kentucky Senator Mitch McConnell. I heard Senator McConnell make his powerful points in a recent radio interview. He started by saying that the American public has already voted by the devastating margin of *nine to one* against public financing. That was his way of framing the claim that only one in ten Americans check the box to direct $3 of their federal tax payment to presidential elections. I'm not sure if his figures are exactly right, or if there's any data showing why people do or don't check the box when they file their taxes. But I wouldn't dispute the point that, as we sit here today, most people don't support public financing.

Senator McConnell went on to say that Americans don't want to use money on campaigns that could be used instead to feed the hungry or help people in other ways. I expect that every one of us could find expenditures in the federal budget that we'd rather see spent helping people. But then he went on to what seemed to be his main point. He said that Americans *really* don't want their money going to candidates they don't like. "That offends them," he said.

Now, that's pretty persuasive — until you start considering what elections are for and about. They are the final step in the process of selecting people to represent us, to make decisions for us in our republic. And we can't select very well without information about the alternative choices. This is where I think Senator McConnell gets it wrong. This isn't about tax dollars going to candidates who taxpayers don't like. It's about those funds going to candidates that they've never heard of (or, if they've heard the names, whose positions and qualifications they don't know). And often the reason that those candidates aren't known — the reason they don't have the privilege of your attention the way that I do today — is that they're not marching in lockstep with the special interests who fund political campaigns. They're independent. They formulate their stands without worrying about what their big campaign contributors will think, because they don't have any. Would you agree with me that in these times of polarization and stalemate among clashing special interests, hearing from this kind of candidate might be a gift as we're trying to decide who should represent us?

The decisions we make in the voting booth have much less value when we don't know the range of possible alternatives. And within the real-world framework of modern American politics, I believe that public campaign financing is the best way, and perhaps the only way, to show us a broad range before we vote. And it's not just a matter of increasing the number of candidates to choose from. What we've learned from people like John Anderson, Ross Perot and John McCain is that the rise of a plainspoken, Emperor-has-no-clothes challenger chases the leading candidates from the shelter of platitudes and comfortable campaign slogans toward some real, accountable talk that gives us better grounds for making our decision. That's what public financing could do, *not for them, but for us.*

Of course, if you'll let me fall back on a platitude myself, the devil is in the details. Although public financing works across Europe in ways that satisfy Europeans, it needs to be carefully developed and refined here. I referred to one of the important design details earlier when I was talking about *"bona fide* candidates." If this is supposed to be a really fair and open process, do we start handing tax dollars to anyone and everyone who call themselves candidate for office? No. Then who decides who's a "real" candidate? We do. One reasonable approach was laid out in a 2000 ballot initiative in my own state of Oregon. To qualify for public funding, a candidate for Governor would have to collect a minimum of 8,000 contributions of $5 each. Secretary of State candidates would need 6,000 five-dollar donations, Attorney General and State Treasurer candidates would need 4,000, state Senators 500 and State Representatives 300 five-dollar donations, with at least 75 percent coming from within their districts. The numbers would have to be adjusted for Congress and the Presidency, but I think the point is clear: anyone with the tenacity and appeal to amass that kind of support probably has something valuable to offer us in a competitive election.

Still, though, there's the expenditure of all those tax dollars. All those dollars that Senator McConnell says could be going somewhere else, to things that Americans really care about. With money tight and budget deficits growing, can we afford to have government take on another new function? There are two answers to that. One is mathematical and the other's practical.

As a matter of arithmetic, the money that went into elections for President and the Congress exceeded $1 billion last cycle. Let's double that to $2 billion and set it next to the $2.164 trillion 2005 federal budget. That's less than 1/10 of one percent of the total. Then remember that the election cycle occurs every two years for Congress and every four years for President, which means that the annual cost of full public financing would be amount to something like one-thirtieth of one percent of the budget.

But that's just arithmetic. Two billion dollars is still enough to help a lot of Americans in a lot of ways. Do we really want to use it to start paying for elections? But *starting to pay* for elections is not what we would be doing, and this may be the most important point of all. We wouldn't be starting because *we are paying for them now.* And we're paying much, much more than $2 billion. What we have in place today is this curiously opaque system where political campaigns are *bought* by narrowly focused special interests and then *paid for* with our tax dollars.

For illustration purposes let's look at just three recent spending decisions. I'll use these because they are fresh in our memories, not because they're unique to this Congress or this White House. We've been paying exorbitantly for our elections for a long time, through the leadership of both major parties.

Congress recently passed a "Medicare reform" bill to provide drug benefits to seniors. When it came to the floor for a vote its price tag was $400 billion. A week later an "adjustment" put the cost at $535 billion. It's been independently estimated that this reform will steer something like $200 billion in additional revenue to the pharmaceutical industry.

Some months earlier Congress passed a $200 billion farm bill that looked like farm bills we see most years, only bigger. Again there's a broad consensus of observers pointing out that a huge slice of that pie will go not to helping family farmers survive, keeping food prices down, helping our balance of trade, or creating jobs, but instead to fattening the bottom line of agribusiness corporations who donate millions to political campaigns.

Then there's the whole world of military spending, which deserves much more attention than we'll give it today. For now I'll sidestep the complex debate of how much this nation really needs to spend on defense in this dangerous world, and say just this: of the $450 billion to $700 billion we will spend on military and related security functions this year, there is consistent agreement among military professionals with no current ties to politics or industry that tens of billions — some would put it at hundreds of billions — will go to projects that will do nothing at all to make

America more powerful or secure.

I'm sure there are different views among us on all three of these issues. But let me ask you this: is there anyone in this room who believes that we wouldn't save much more than $2 billion if the men and women voting on these budgets no longer had to answer to their biggest campaign contributors? That's why you and I are paying much more for elections today than we would under public campaign financing. Since we're already paying, wouldn't it be better if we were the buyers-of-record of our political races, the real owners of this government?

A few moments ago I was suggesting that what knocks our process off-track is one powerful question at critical decision-making moments: *What will my big contributors think about this?* It might be unrealistic to believe we'll ever eliminate that question. Maybe we don't need to. Maybe we don't even want to. With public financing in place, it might be exactly the right question to ask, because those "big contributors" would be you and me and everyone we know, *all* of us who are supposed to be equally represented in a democratic republic. *That* would work. Because we pay for them directly, they would be our campaigns. Our politics. Our elections. Finally, blessedly... our nation.

Thank you very much.

★ ★ ★ ★ ★

The discussion guide for this speech is on page 133.

Two

On the Contrary...

*Telling the Automobile Association of America
the Price of Gasoline is Too Low*

Ladies and Gentlemen,

I've been listening carefully to my opponents in this forum, especially as they've responded to your concern about the rising price of gasoline. You've said this is becoming a serious financial burden for you. I'll take you at your word on that. The cost of keeping our vehicles running is a growing slice of the pie of most Americans' household budgets at the same time that other slices are increasing. Meanwhile the whole pie isn't getting any bigger. You have the sense that something has to give here, and I think you're right. So you ask us what we would do as President to lower or at least stabilize the price of gasoline.

And you've heard my opponents answer. _____ on my right here says we should ease environmental restrictions on exploration and drilling for more oil, and adjust the tax code to make drilling more attractive. On my left, _____ says he wants to explore and drill the private records of the major oil companies to see if they're colluding to boost their profit margins with higher prices at the pump.

So now it's my turn. My plan for lowering the price of gasoline at the pump is... I don't have a plan. Not because I haven't thought about it, but because my goal is not cheaper gasoline. I don't believe that goal is good for America. I'll go further than that. If we can expand this conversation beyond the immediate future, I don't believe cheaper gas is good even for the millions of Americans who are feeling a painful wallop every time they pull up to the gas pump.

Let's do a sound check here. Did you just hear me say I'm not in favor of keeping gasoline prices as low as possible? Can a candidate for President of the United States actually say that and stay in the race? Well, bear with me for the next few minutes and let's find out.

Let me start by telling you why I'm here at all. Running for President is an expensive, hugely demanding process. No thoughtful person decides to do it lightly. The decision process caused me to probe my beliefs about the world more deeply and broadly than I ever have. I had to articulate for myself the *core* of what I believe about America and my role and responsibilities as an American. What I was looking for was a *practical touchstone* to keep my direction true, a simple guiding principle I could bring to the brutally difficult decisions Presidents are called upon to make day after day. I have found that touchstone, and it comes in the form of a question that I will ask myself at the moment of every major decision. It is this question:

Of the choices available to me here, which one is best for my children and their children?

This is actually a modern abbreviation of the creed that some tribal cultures have lived by for centuries. You've probably heard the phrase "Seventh Generation." It's been popularized to a point where one large manufacturer of paper and household cleaning products has taken it for its company name. You might know that it had special meaning for some Native American people who believed their decisions should be based on the impact they will have on their descendants seven generations into the future. Seven generations! Counting you and me as the first generation, that means we would be basing our actions today on how they'll affect our great-great-great-great grandchildren. Or to move in the other direction, it would be as if our ancestors in about 1850, ten years before the Civil War, were specifically worrying about you and me when they made decisions together.

Is that a concept you can fully grasp? I can't. Imagining how our behavior today will ripple out over that much time is more than my brain is wired to do. Maybe Native Americans really knew how to do it. But very few of us are Native Americans. We are who we are, and we have the cultural and mental resources that we have. So let's not commit ourselves to planning seven generations out. But how about . . . *three?*

Planning for the Third Generation means planning for our grandchildren, and that doesn't take a gifted imagination. For some of us, those little people are already here. We lift them onto our laps and tickle them and spoil them (actually, for some of us they don't fit on our laps anymore, and we haven't tickled them for a long time; some of your grandchildren may even have children of their own). Some of you don't have grandchildren, but I'll bet there are very little people crawling around somewhere who you love. Those are the people we're talking about.

All I want to know is this: are we willing to commit ourselves to them? That's the question you should be asking your candidates, and it's the question we should be asking you. Are you willing to do what it takes to pass a healthy, thriving world on to our grandchildren?

Don't answer too quickly. I'm asking here for more than noble words and intentions. Committing ourselves to our grandchildren means making adjustments and taking action. We can start with the issue that's in front of us right this minute. When it comes to policies that will affect what you and I pay at the gas pump, I invite you to ask the decisive question with me: *Of the choices available here, which one is best for our children and their children?*

Is it to keep gasoline as inexpensive as we can? I don't think so. That serves *our* needs, certainly. It lets us continue to hop into our own cars and trucks all by ourselves and drive absolutely wherever we want absolutely whenever we want. That is absolutely wonderful — for us. But we're the First Generation. Right now we're exploring the best choices for the Second and Third. What does keeping gasoline inexpensive do for them?

It might be easier to answer that question if we could take a little field trip. Imagine that at 5:30 this afternoon we were standing together on an overpass of a freeway on the outskirts of almost any major city in our country, looking down at the traffic below us. We would be looking at the tops of more vehicles than we could count, traveling in both directions. The details would vary from city to city, but here's something that we'd likely see anywhere: a solid sea of cars and trucks, separated from one another by a very few feet of pavement, shuffling away from the city in three or four mile-per-hour bursts, all in a galaxy of blinking brake lights stretching off into the distance as far as we could see. With just a little less movement, what we'd be seeing would be a very long, narrow, completely full parking lot with sparkling red lights.

And if we looked more carefully, we might see something else. We might notice that a large majority of these slowly creeping vehicles, perhaps as many as four out of five, are carrying one person. I don't mean one person alongside the driver; I mean the one person who *is* the driver.

If we can step back from the haze of our daily habits, this is really quite a picture: two to four lines of autos that disappear over the horizon, most of them with one lonely person and plenty of empty seats inside, each of them burning up gasoline or diesel as they idle in place, waiting for the chance to advance a few feet at a time. And we're not talking about a single moment in a single city. This happens on hundreds of highways across the nation, and it happens twice a day, five days a week — seven days, in some metropolitan areas — every week of the year, year after year after year.

And if we were standing together watching all this from our perch on the overpass, no matter what your political persuasion or your views on the environment or your faith in industrial technology to solve our problems, I would have to ask you: is this working? Can this possibly be the best choice to make for our kids and their kids?

No, it's not. There at least three big reasons.

1. It pumps more greenhouse gasses in the air than just about any system we could devise for getting us from point A to point B. If we remember our view from the overpass, we know that even as we sit in stationary cars going nowhere at all, we're converting tanker-loads of oil into carbon dioxide.

2. It commits our grandkids to trillions of dollars of ineffective transportation spending in the form of highway maintenance that never quite keeps up and road expansions to add yet one more lane that will *also* clog up with cars in a matter of months. That will mean trillions of dollars that won't be available for any of their other public needs, like paying off the multi-trillion dollar national debt we're already handing to our grandchildren. And

3. It creates a thirst for more and more gasoline and diesel that can only be satisfied with more expensive drilling in more and more environmentally fragile areas, or more aggressive and budget-busting military postures towards oil-producing nations, or both.

Can we continue all of this and still claim to be truly committed to our grandchildren? I don't think so. I say we owe it to them to move beyond tender words about what they mean to us and start building transportation systems that will get them from A to B much more sensibly and efficiently than the one we have today. We owe them the first steps towards systems they can use for their lifetimes without spending so much that there's nothing left over for their other needs.

The very good news is that we don't have to invent most of those systems. Other countries of the world, countries where people are used to affluence and comfort much like ours, already have. I'm talking about everything from high-speed passenger train travel between cities to bus, trolley and small jitney routes within them, from friendlier surroundings for pedestrians and bicycles to effective, wide-reaching programs to stagger work schedules and assemble car pools. I'm talking about systems that have matured to work magnificently in places that we visit all over the world, plus a couple of surprises here and there that new technologies are likely to offer us.

With a few localized exceptions, we haven't advanced these transportation systems for our grandkids very far because we haven't had to. And we haven't had to for one reason and one reason only: cheap gasoline. Cheap, that is, if you look only at the portion of the price that comes out of our personal wallets today. The remainder of that price — the public health bills from the emissions of those slowly moving rush-hour parking lots we were talking about, the incalculable costs of climate change down the road, a cluster of environmental costs as we drill in more marginal places, and the military costs of keeping foreign oil flowing at friendly prices, all of those hidden add-ons to the official price we pay at the pump — none of that has wholly registered with us. With little or no thought, we're adding those costs to the big tab we're already handing to our children and their children to pay. Any fair judge of what we've been *doing* here, as compared to what we've been *saying*, would think that we don't give a damn about our grandkids.

What a fair judge would see is two things: number one, the gasoline we use today is subsidized by our kids and grandkids down to a price cheap enough to let us side-step the inconvenience of shifting to new systems that would work well years from now. And number two, years from now our grandkids will receive a supplementary bill for the gas we're burning today, along with a collapsed transportation system that they can't escape, because their grandparents side-stepped the work of developing serious alternatives.

Once more, please: *Of the choices available here, which one is best for our children and their children?* Would you agree there are better answers to that question than keeping gasoline prices down right now? These answers will take clear vision and the courage to say no to politically potent groups that profit enormously from maintaining today's conditions.

Before I suggest five choices that would serve our grandchildren much better over time, we have a cold reality to face right now in the near term. For millions of Americans today, sharply rising gas prices wouldn't mean irritation or inconvenience — they would mean serious hardship. These are people who have few if any other alternatives for getting to and from sub-living wage jobs, or from their rural homes to medical and other services in town. Some are teetering on the financial edge right now and this extra cost could push them off into real despair. We can't let that happen. The changes I'm about to outline won't take place overnight, and we can't take from these people their only realistic means of getting to work and doing their essential business. If gasoline prices start reflecting real costs, we have to protect them with transitional programs. These might include coupons on the order of food stamps, networks of public van routes, non-profit service grants to get more people car-pooling, and new solutions that creative people will develop in their own communities.

I don't want to minimize the challenge of this transition. It won't be simple. But if we're honestly committed to the Third Generation, there has to be a bigger picture at the center of our vision. The new path I'll describe has risks and uncertainties. But the path we're on now, based on the evidence of our eyes and ears, the projections of scientists from different disciplines, and the vectors of politics and struggle in oil-rich parts of the world, leads straight over a cliff.

If you're on a wagon galloping towards the edge of a cliff, getting off is going to be difficult and probably scary. One way to hide from the fear is to argue about how far off the cliff really is, since no one knows for sure. But the closer you get to the cliff, the harder and more dangerous the jumping becomes. When you're right at the edge and can see clearly down into the void, it's too late. You're over the edge, and you get to spend the free-fall regretting and wondering — wondering why you didn't jump when you could.

But jump to where? Here are five possible parts of a choice that's much better for our grandchildren than the one we're making now.

1. Vital mass transportation in every American city and most American towns, with large buses and trolleys on high-density routes, small vans going out into the suburbs and beyond, all in patterns designed by local people who know their communities. We'll use federal gas taxes and perhaps some surcharges to match the efforts of local governments that want to build great public transit systems, with extra incentives for alternative energy vehicles.

2. Conversion of a fraction of America's weapons and munitions manufacturing capacity to new generations of high-efficiency trains to carry people within and between cities. Here we start with the advantage of existing factories, expertise and labor forces that know how to produce huge, new-technology machines. Let's stop building multi-billion dollar weapons systems that military experts say we'll never use and start building trams and trains at least as useful as the ones that transport millions of Europeans and Japanese every day.

3. Start-up funding for new businesses to establish car-pooling and ride-sharing programs that copy the best practices around and make them even better, so that the same number of people get where they need to go with far fewer cars on the road.

4. Tax incentives for businesses that help reduce traffic congestion with strategies like staggered work shifts and telecommuting.

5. Assistance for local and state governments to develop long-term land use planning that prompts more people to walk, bicycle or drive shorter distances to their work.

Will all this be expensive? Of course it will. But no more than we're spending to prop up today's system, and perhaps much less. Will it involve major government subsidies? There's no doubt about it — subsidies that will give our kids and grandkids a much better shot at functional cities and towns than the big, less obvious government subsidies we're paying for today. Will we get enough bang from every dollar spent? Of course not. We're taking a new fork in the road here. We can't possibly know how well all these changes will work. We'll design them the best we can on the front end and watch them closely to make the course corrections we need.

There are political experts, people I respect, who say that no one who asks for this kind of change from Americans can be a serious presidential contender. We love our cars too much, they say, especially the ability they give us to hop in them at any time of any day and go exactly where we want with whom we want by any route we want. That's not hard for me to understand; one of the people all of that describes is me. I bought my first car with savings from paper routes and grocery jobs when I was 18. I've had one or more ever since. I'm used to that absolute freedom of movement, and the thought of limiting it doesn't fill my heart with joy. It's so tempting to hold on to this delicious privilege, to support and vote for whatever it takes to keep gasoline as cheap as possible for as long as possible, and distract ourselves from pondering the consequences too closely. It is so easy to do that. You all know what we tell ourselves:

Do I care about my grandkids? Are you kidding? They mean the world to me. And the impacts of all this business on them? Well, hell, I don't know the impacts, I'm no fortune-teller. Things will work out for them down the road somehow. I'm sure they will ...

No. Let's not do that. If you'll step up with me to commit to the Third Generation — if you're really ready to base our choices on what's best for our children and grandchildren — let's start now by demanding much more of our leaders than a promise to keep prices down at the corner gas pump.

Thank you.

★ ★ ★ ★ ★

The discussion guide for this speech is on page 134.

Three

"No Amount is Too Much..."

Telling the Veterans of Foreign Wars
Military Spending is Too high

Good afternoon, and thanks for the opportunity to speak to you this afternoon.

With Veterans Day just behind us, I want to begin by saying that I'm deeply grateful to you. I never served in the armed forces. That doesn't keep me from knowing that many of the privileges I enjoy as a American, including and especially the privilege to speak my mind as I see fit, are made possible by a strong military presence in the world. That's why I want to use the short time I have with you today to talk about national security. I am deeply concerned about America's national security. I believe that we're becoming less secure because of our current level of military spending.

Do you agree? Well, let me be more specific. In my judgment our military budget is too big to protect the security of this nation. If we want to be genuinely secure, we have to spend less money. I will say that again: *if we want America to be secure, we have to spend less than we do today for military purposes.* I hope you'll bear with me for a few minutes to see if that could be true.

The logical place to start is to establish how much we're spending right now. As it happens that's not a simple matter. The amount falls somewhere between four hundred and fifty and seven hundred billion dollars. Where you land within that range depends on what you choose to count. The official budget for the Pentagon, the sub-total for that agency you'll find printed in the massive document that is trucked from the Capitol Building to the White House for signature, comes in at the lower number. That's where some want to stop counting. But that's not an honest place to stop.

There are several places in the federal budget *outside* of the Pentagon's section where you'll find expenditures that a reasonable person would call military spending. One is the Department of Energy, which has responsibilities for monitoring, maintaining, and protecting America's nuclear weapons arsenal. For some reason those billions of dollars are not generally considered part of military spending. And the Department of Homeland Security will spend more billions on functions that are plainly part of our overall military structure.

Yet another fifty billion dollars will be spent by the Department of Veterans Affairs. That they are dollars well-spent doesn't change the fact that they are made necessary by our military activities. And if you hold military spending responsible for its share of the national debt — something the budget-writers have never done — you need to add almost a hundred and forty billion dollars more to the tab for interest payments.

Even if the budget bureaucrats were to fall into a seizure of fiscal honesty and include those as military costs, we would still have to deal with the shell-games of their political bosses before we arrive at the true total. Nowadays it seems as if generally accepted accounting practices fly out the window when the actual shooting starts. As the recent war in Iraq deepened and lengthened, a few people noticed that *not one* of the hundreds of billions of dollars that it cost was included in the annual budget that the President sent to Capitol Hill. Can I tell you what the President's budget staff said when they were asked about this little omission? They left out the cost of the war, they said, *because they didn't know exactly what the final number would be.*

That's correct. Because they couldn't know exactly how much the war would cost, the amount of money our leaders assigned to it in the federal budget — the budget debated and passed by the Congress, signed by the President, and offered to the American people as the outline of how our resources will be spent — was zero. Zero dollars and zero cents.

What great news that could be for every one of us who have to make budgets for our businesses or households. If you budget like this, you can make the cost of your car or truck for the next year nothing at all, zero dot zero zero, because there's no way to know exactly how much you'll have to spend. That's right. You get to own, fuel, drive, maintain and repair your vehicle for free for the next twelve months!

This sleight-of-hand from Washington D.C. tells me plainly that the leaders of our country know we're spending too much on the military, or at least more than Americans would accept if we had all the facts. This is just one of many reasons over time, and through different presidencies, that our military spending in the real world ends up to be greater, often much greater, than official documents and public debate say that it is. That is a hard fact of modern politics that we have to keep in mind if we really want to find the smartest level of military spending for this country.

Once all of this is factored in, a solid case can be made that our annual military bill actually comes close to seven hundred billion dollars. But for the sake of our discussion today let's pick a lower number. Let's say we're only spending five hundred billion, half a trillion, tax dollars for military purposes. I have to pause to catch my breath here; I never thought the phrase "only half a trillion dollars" would ever pass my lips. If you asked the bank to let you have that in crisp new one dollar bills, you'd walk out with a stack about twenty miles high.

But then it is a dangerous world, and no sensible person would say national security comes cheap. So let's consider this: if we spent a full trillion dollars, would we be twice as secure? Would spending two trillion dollars make us four times as secure? Would fifty trillion dollars make America one hundred times more secure than we are today?

That's an absurd way of thinking about security, wouldn't you agree? But it flows naturally from what our leaders are telling us today. When the President is asked about a military budget that is bigger than ever and growing by the week, he says "No amount is too much when it comes to protecting America's security." Well, yes, but does that answer the question? He could use the exact same words if military spending jumped up to one trillion or two trillion or fifty trillion dollars: "No amount is too much when it comes to protecting America's security. "

How many of you would call yourselves fiscal conservatives? [pause]

Good. I'm glad to see all those hands. They tell me I'm in the right company. One of the things I expect from government is accountability for how it spends my money. I think we owe that much to our children and their children now more than ever, because at this point we're already leaving them with over seven trillion dollars of our IOUs to pay off. Are we doing our job when we accept "No amount is too much when it comes to protecting America's security " as an explanation of the military budget?

Let's bring this closer to home. Do you remember that car we just talked about, the one you figured will cost you nothing to run in the next year because you don't know exactly how much it will cost you to run? Let's say you discover that its brakes are shot and you take it into the corner repair shop. When you come to pick it up the mechanic hands you a bill for $10,000. You get up off the floor and ask him how that could possibly be. He looks you in the eye, puts a hand on your shoulder and says "I don't think any amount is too much to make sure you and your family are safe on the road, do you?" Would that satisfy you? It's satisfying the nation when the Mechanic-in-Chief says it.

Now, anyone who lays all the responsibility for this whopping bill at the President's door isn't paying attention. Some weapons systems have become such obvious white elephants in today's world that the Pentagon has wanted to discontinue them. They're also willing to close military bases that have outlived their purpose. We keep funding some of these useless weapons and bases not because of the President, but because they pour money into communities and fatten military contracts that are important to key members of Congress. When those members are challenged on especially wasteful examples, they'll sometimes say what the President does — "No amount is too much," and so on and so forth — but more often they'll talk about the jobs their constituents would lose if those programs were cut.

When they say that, I pay attention. I think they're talking about a real problem. I want to ask them if they think the only way to protect their people from financial disaster is to produce weapons and services that are useless at best, needlessly provocative to other countries of the world at worst, and in either case wasteful of all kinds of valuable resources. I don't buy that and I don't think you should either.

The excess manufacturing capacity of the military industry isn't a problem. It's a great asset that can help us solve some big

problems ahead of us, from relieving the miserable traffic congestion of our cities with new generations of buses and trains to making new forms of clean energy much more affordable. Before too
long that could mean more jobs, and more *fruitful, truly useful
jobs*, than the inefficient part of the military industry provides
today. That's a topic worth pursuing in a separate discussion.

For now let's put the focus back on that five hundred billion
dollars, the very lowest number you could assign to the military
budget. How can we put that figure into perspective? Well, one
thing we know is that amounts to more than the military spending of all of the other countries on planet Earth *combined*. That's
correct. If you add the costs of all the armies, navies, air forces,
marines and special forces of all of the two hundred-plus
nations of the world that are not the United States, and then add
on all the weapons, supplies and bureaucracies needed to support them, you end up with a sum that is smaller than our country's military spending. Whatever your political views, will you
think about that with me for a brief moment? [pause]

I have to ask you: does this make sense? It can make sense
only to someone who believes that America's best path to security is to stand as a permanent full-time, fully armed, fully
armored police force able to head off or quickly crush every
attack, assassination, kidnaping, riot, bombing, gassing, land-
mine and firefight that erupts at any time or place in the world.
This model says that we'll rout any enemy if we apply enough
forceful suppression, and that if we're not winning, well, that
must mean we haven't applied enough force.

Perhaps there was a time when that was possible. The
Romans prevailed for a while with that model, until their military machine sucked the lifeblood from their whole society. But
when you look at today's world — the world as it actually is

today, not as we wish it would be — how could that work? Today a single person can kill hundreds by wrapping him or herself in a few pounds of inexpensive, undetectable explosives. He or she can kill thousands with chemicals or germs that are not difficult to acquire. It may now be possible for one or two people to fire off a nuclear weapon from a shoulder-mounted launcher. Combine these technical means with a growing number of people in the world eagerly willing to die for their version of Truth and Righteousness and it becomes hard to give credence to the thesis that we can secure America by force and violence alone.

There are other candidates who would stand with me to say that outspending the rest of the world combined won't ultimately make us secure. But I'm saying more than that. I'm saying that spending that much of our wealth makes us *less* secure. There are two reasons.

The first is that the choice to support this level of military spending is effectively a choice not to support other essential ingredients of national security. Former Senator Mark Hatfield of Oregon often challenged his colleagues to examine what makes a nation genuinely secure. He didn't deny that a well-armed military was part of it. But he made us ask ourselves if a nation where millions of people have no access to the kind of education that leads to worthwhile jobs is really secure. In the last few years, more and more young Americans are finding universities and even community colleges out of their reach. He made us ask if a nation where millions go to bed hungry each night is really secure. More and more Americans are going to bed hungry. He asked if a nation where families can lose everything they've saved when a family member falls ill is really secure. That's exactly what has happened to many Americans. Ultimately I think his question was this: *when growing numbers of Americans don't feel as if they have any real stake in the society, can America as a nation be secure?* He said that we can't, and I agree.

The decision to fund the military at current levels is very literally a decision to do little or nothing about those other elements of security. That's the news that has greeted the nation's governors when they go to Washington. Coming from states that are suffering through fiscal nightmares, the governors visit the White House to beg for help to keep their schools and health clinics open, to keep police on the highways, to keep from releasing criminals early (remember that governors are required to balance their budgets, which is not a concept that the President and Congress seem to be familiar with). They are turned down flat. The President tells them he'd like to help, he really would, but he can't — because the money's all gone. Half a trillion dollars of it has gone to a military budget greater than the sum total of all the rest of the world's military budgets. I suggest to you that when we have schools and clinics closing, streets and highways without police, criminals who are discovering they *can* do the crime without doing the time, we do not have a secure nation. You don't have to do any more than walk the streets of most American cities to know that's true.

To understand the second way this much military spending undercuts our security, you'd want to take your walk in other parts of the world. Much of the spending goes to maintain a U.S. military presence in over 140 countries around the world. It's vital to try to grasp the impact in those countries, either by going there yourself or checking international media sources; relying entirely on U.S. media makes it almost impossible to make heads or tails of the attitudes toward America around the world. If we could visit these countries or watch stories together from the most respected news organizations in the world, we would see a whole lot of people actively unhappy with our country. Why is that? I'm sure that in this room we'd come up with very different answers to that question. And we've unwisely let those disagreements over what happened in the past distract us from a clear-headed look at what the American military should be in the present. We can't afford to do that anymore.

Let's agree that there's no single reason for the international hostility towards America. There are several. One is surely the work of ultra-religious zealots who manipulate people for their own agendas. But we have to ask why they find so many people so receptive to their message. I believe it's because the face of America that they see is very different from the one we see every day. What they see are uniformed squads of soldiers rolling around their country in humvees and armored personnel carriers. From time to time they see uprisings that pit American soldiers against their neighbors and friends and even their children.

We have to ask how that affects their children, youngsters growing up in abject poverty who rarely see Americans who aren't wearing camouflage and helmets and powerful automatic weapons. If that's their whole exposure to Americans, while adults around them are constantly urging them to take pride in their country and in their religious tradition, what are they most likely to believe? Who do these children grow up to be? I believe that honest answers to those questions bring us to the probability that much of our military spending abroad is making America less secure.

If we want real security it's time to show those countries a different face of America. It's time to show them our generosity. What would happen if we shifted dollars from tanks, aircraft carriers and landmines into rural development, water and sanitation projects, literacy and skills training and small business incubation, all designed to help them build strong local economies? We'd do that not so that people around the world would praise our generosity, but for a practical reason. We would do it because we know from history's lessons, in other countries just as in our own, that strong local economies *give people a stake in their future.* People with a stake in their own future do not fly planes into buildings, strap plastic explosives to their bodies, or cook up deadly chemical or biological weapons in secret warehouses.

Many in this room have the personal experience to know this is true. Many of you fought for military victory over Germany and Japan. Then you came home and supported the rebuilding of those countries through the Marshall Plan, which turned two of our bitterest enemies into two of our best friends and trading partners. That generous plan of redevelopment and investment absolutely made our country more secure. It proved that lasting security calls for more than the military power to overcome today's armed threats.

If half a trillion dollars is too much military spending for our national security, what's the right amount? Honest people who agree that the world's a dangerous place and who want our money spent efficiently will come up with different answers. Here is the main question I've come here to ask: would you be willing to help find a number? One of my first acts as your President will be to convene an independent panel to review the current military budgets program-by-program for effectiveness and relevance to today's real needs. That panel should have members from the ranks of retired military officers and analysts, from taxpayer watchdog associations, and from groups with expertise in international affairs and negotiation. I also want representation from the Veterans of Foreign Wars, both because of the commitment you've already demonstrated to national security and the on-the-ground experience you would bring to the table. Would you be willing to serve your country again?

Until I'm given the authority to create that panel, I want to issue another kind of call. I won't ask you to add your voice to those who want 20 or 50 or 100 billion dollars sliced from military spending. You'd first want to know the details and consequences, and that's fair. What I'm asking from you as fellow fiscal conservatives is to break free of this hare-brained "no price is too high" slogan and demand accountability from your government for more than a half trillion dollars funneled to military uses this year, the exact same accountability you want applied to health care, welfare or job training programs. You are entitled to that. We all are.

Thank you.

★ ★ ★ ★ ★

The discussion guide for this speech is on page 135.

Four

To Secure the Blessings of Liberty

Telling the Christian Coalition of America
Gay Marriage Should Not Be Banned

Thank you for inviting me here today to share my views on same-sex marriage, and how government should fit into the picture. I know it's a vital issue for you, and you deserve straight answers. I'm not sure you're getting them from most candidates right now. You'll hear those in my own party offering a well-honed position: they're for civil unions to make sure homosexual couples enjoy the same basic domestic partnership rights that others do, but that doesn't make them for gay marriage. Marriage, they say, should be reserved for the union of a man and a woman.

Here's what I think about that position. I think it has one main purpose: to satisfy you, or at least keep your angry opposition to a manageable level. Does it? It wouldn't satisfy me if I shared your belief that gay marriage should be banned. I may be missing something here — you should never discount that possibility with me — but it sounds like a tactic to get out of harm's way rather than an honest and authentic belief. This is clever word play, not conviction. I believe some candidates, listening harder than they should to their pollsters, are trying to thread a tiny needle to a place of safety on this intensely divisive issue.

I won't do that. I don't want anyone leaving here today

unclear on my views on amending the United States Constitution to ban same-sex marriage. I'm completely against that proposal. I really don't expect to leave here with converts to my point of view, but I want you to know exactly where I stand and why.

I start with the document that some are anxious to change. What's the United States Constitution all about? We don't have to wonder. It has a Preamble that tells us.

> "We the people of the United States, in order to form a more perfect union, establish justice, insure domestic tranquility, provide for the common defense, promote the general welfare, and secure the blessings of liberty to ourselves and our posterity, do ordain and establish this Constitution for the United States of America."

Beautiful words, aren't they? And at the same time not very specific. The Framers might have wanted it that way, but one outcome of their work is that honest people can read different practical meanings into those noble words. More than "can;" people read very different meanings into the Constitution every day. These words leave room for me to argue that anything in life that I deeply care about has a place in the Constitution, because anything I deeply care about certainly relates to "domestic tranquility," to our "general welfare" and absolutely, without a shadow of a doubt, to "forming a more perfect union." So because I know you believe deeply that marriage should be the exclusive domain of one man coming together with one woman, I understand how you'd see this amendment fitting into our Constitution.

When I say I *understand*, I am saying that I get it with my head. To be honest with you, I do *not* get it with my heart. I have tried again and again to grasp the belief that when two consenting, mentally competent people of the same sex choose to marry, and the state recognizes that choice with a license, one result will be damage to *your* marriage, or, if you're single, to a marriage you may choose in the future. Or that it threatens in any concrete way our general welfare or quest for a more perfect union. I could ask you one more time to explain it to me, but I'm pretty certain that after you did I'd still be scratching my head. And I guess that you'd end up scratching your head in puzzlement that I don't understand.

What this tells me is that ultimately this is not an issue for the brain. It's not a matter where the reasoning process helps very much, like, say, a debate over health care reform or foreign aid might be. It is a deeper matter than that, a matter of the heart. A matter, if you will, of *faith*. And that's not to minimize it in any way; your faith deserves as much respect as your rational thoughts do.

What your faith does *not* deserve, and what my faith does not deserve, is the enforcement power of the United States Constitution. The Founding Fathers, who disagreed on so much, shared a belief that the Constitution shouldn't shape a government according to the tenets of *anyone's* faith — that in fact much of its purpose is to protect those who don't subscribe to popular or mainstream faiths.

Now, I wasn't there. I have no inkling of what George Washington, Thomas Jefferson, James Madison or Alexander Hamilton, all deeply religious men, thought of homosexuality, or even if the subject crossed their minds. But I absolutely believe that any of them standing here today would tell us that a federal prohibition on marriage between people of the same sex does not belong in the document they created for us.

I suppose we could leave it at that. You could ask me if I'll support a constitutional amendment to ban gay marriage, I say no, and we go about our separate ways. There are candidates who *like* to leave it right there, as an almost lawyerly debate of what does and doesn't belong in the United States Constitution, so they don't have to handle the red-hot core of this issue. They will say that a ban like this doesn't belong in the Constitution and that anything like it should come from the states instead, hoping you'll leave it at that. I don't want to leave it at that.

I do agree with them that this is properly a state matter. We've always assigned authority over social institutions like marriage to the states, and I haven't heard one persuasive argument to change that foundational practice now. But I don't want to use my agreement on the technical point as a conversation-closer, hoping you won't probe my personal beliefs any further. I'm not here to hide behind a narrow political scientist's argument. If we're going to stand before you and ask for your vote, you deserve to know our core personal principles. You should ask a follow-up question: if a law banning gay marriage were on the table in my state, would I support it?

No, I wouldn't. If this proposal comes to the ballot in my state or a legislator asks me about it, I won't be shy to share my opinion that it's a bad trade. It would curb personal freedom without offering the counterbalancing public benefit we should expect when we curb freedom. And if a majority of people in my state agree more with you than with me, I may have to live with an outcome I don't like. It wouldn't be the first time.

So this goes beyond what I believe our Constitution is all about. It goes to what I believe our *nation* is all about. It is about one of those promises our ancestors gave us in the Preamble I read a moment ago: "to secure the blessings of liberty for ourselves and our posterity."

This nation is about securing our blessings of liberty, both from enemies abroad and from those whose beliefs are so strong that they want everyone to adopt them. We all know our personal liberties aren't absolute. They are limited every day by the rules for driving on the road, by the rights of others to keep their private property, by our neighbors' rights to live in a quiet safe place. But here's what I take to be at the very center of what this country's about: *we compromise individual liberties only when we must in order to protect the rights and well-being of others.*

When we take away a man's liberty to marry a man, or a woman's to marry a woman, do we meet that test? You may say "yes." You may tell me that the knowledge that two people of the same sex have married, no matter how private and quiet they may be, degrades the institution of marriage in a way that deeply affects your mental or spiritual well-being. If you say that, I will believe you. But if that's the bar at which we start restricting personal freedoms, we're on our way to a very different America than the one our forefathers promised — a very different America than the one that you and I enjoy in fact today.

As we sit here at this moment there's music playing with lyrics that harm the mental well-being of some people. At this very moment there are paintings and sculptures upsetting others. There are movies and magazines and ethnic jokes and clothing styles and reading material and religious beliefs and huge SUVs cruising down the highway that are causing people real distress. It could be I'm hurting someone's mental well-being with the words I'm speaking right now. And this isn't imaginary damage. We are talking about real damage to the mental state of some people subjected to any of these things.

Please understand that I don't mean to minimize the depth of your faith, or the offensiveness of homosexuality to you, by lumping it in with other things that may seem trivial to you by comparison. My only point is this: in my vision of America, the distress that we feel *because of our attitudes or personal faith* — as opposed to the distress we feel when someone steals our car or our pension fund, knocks us over the head with a stick, vandalizes our home, or builds a rock-and-roll nightclub next door — can't serve as a reason to take personal choices away from other people. That's simply not what the Framers of the Constitution that many of you want to amend had in mind.

And so I leave you today with no illusions that I've found the magic words that will move any of you towards my perspective on gay marriage. We're not going to agree. But I also leave you with a promise: just as I stand against this proposed amendment, I will fight any attempt to amend our Constitution, or to pass any law, that compromises your rights or freedoms, unless your use of those freedoms clearly and materially damages other people. And that's not just an imaginary situation. There are people upset enough about Evangelical Christianity that they would remove some of your programs from the airwaves. I would fight a ban like that. There are others who would pass laws to block any presentation of Creation Theory along with Evolution in our public schools. But while some people are offended by Creation Theory, I don't think anyone's shown that teaching it along with Evolution does damage to anyone or violates their rights. So we shouldn't be fiddling with the Constitution or laws in order to stop it.

There are prices we pay for living in a nation genuinely dedicated to personal freedom. One of the highest prices is the turmoil we sometimes feel — the *torment*, for some — because of the behavior or expression of others who live and believe so differently from us. To me, it's a fair price to pay in order to *"secure the blessings of liberty to ourselves and our posterity."* I believe you've demonstrated that blessing today by listening carefully to a viewpoint that might deeply conflict with your own. I'm grateful for that, and I thank you.

★ ★ ★ ★ ★

The discussion guide for this speech is on page 136.

Five
What Does it Symbolize?

Telling the American Legion
Flag Burning Should Be Legal

Thanks for inviting me to join you today, and for offering me a
chance to express my gratitude for the extraordinary ways
that you've served this country. Your invitation specifically
asked me to describe my position on amending the United States
Constitution to make the burning of the American flag a crime.
I am completely against that idea. I appreciate having this
opportunity to tell you why.

I want to start by speaking directly to those of you who
served in combat. I know that some of you have been on the
field of battle with a flag just like the one behind me — probably not as clean and fresh as this one, but right there in full sight
for all to see. I also know that on those battlefields, some of you
took serious wounds, and some of you had beloved friends die
near you in agony, probably within a few feet of a flag like this
one — a flag that might have reminded them, in the last moment
of their lives, what they were fighting for.

After that experience you came home to times of turbulence
in America, especially in reaction to wars in Vietnam and more
recently in Iraq. You may have read about, or watched on TV,
protests where people doused *this same flag with gasoline and*

set a match to it, waving the flames and smoke around in the air as if they were some kind of heroes.

How must that feel to you? I have an idea, a bit of logic in my head about it, but I can't feel it in my heart. I have never been in combat. I don't know how anyone who's never been in full combat, whether or not they've seen the opening scenes of *Saving Private Ryan,* can imagine how it was for you. I never saw what you saw, or lost the friends that you lost. If I say I know how it must feel, I'm not telling the truth.

But I don't need that experience to understand why many of you, along with many Americans who've never seen combat, would like the Constitution amended to make the burning of this flag a crime. Congress has debated the idea plenty of times and I'm sure they will again, maybe in their next session. When they do, I will be standing up in opposition. I'll be saying, with the greatest possible respect for what you have given to this country, that people who burn the American flag should not be punished in any way by their government.

Now, I wonder if that sounds like double-talk to you, thanking you one moment for what you've given America and siding with those who heap scorn on you the next. For me those two thoughts fit together perfectly. I oppose this ban *because* of what you've done, not in spite of it. More than anything else, this is what I've come today to ask you to consider.

What I'm thanking you for is enduring physical and emotional hardships I've only read about, for ultimately putting your lives on the line, to defend the freedoms that I have enjoyed every day of my life as an American citizen — especially my *freedom of expression.* I have grown up knowing that I can express any opinion I want, no matter how silly or ignorant or ugly it may be, about my government and my nation's way of life, without being arrested, jailed, or stripped of my rights or possessions. People in precious few countries throughout history have had that privilege. And you are the ones who have preserved it for me.

Plenty of nations throughout history have *claimed* to be free. Almost all of them have, in fact. But how should that claim be measured? By watching what happens when someone expresses opinions that have nothing to do with the interests of the rulers and the powerful forces in the society? That's obviously not it. By that measure, Hitler, Stalin and Pol Pot could have called their countries free. Is it by seeing what happens to people who politely question what their rulers are doing, taking care that powerful people won't be too offended? That kind of society is better than what Hitler and Stalin gave their people, but it's not good enough for us. I don't believe it's what you fought and watched your friends die for.

What you have protected for us is much more than that. It is a society without those cautious boundaries. It isn't merely a place where we say "Feel free to express anything you want about America anywhere from point A over here to point J over there, because starting at point K some people get really offended, and we can't have that." It is a nation that shows to the world what our Founders had in mind when they approved the First Amendment of the United States Constitution.

If they could be part of our conversation today, they'd tell us they didn't write that amendment to provide for polite debate, or even spirited differences of opinion; we don't need a First Amendment when everyone is behaving. They wrote it, and we need it, *to protect the most obnoxious and insulting forms of expression* — forms of expression, that is to say, like the burning of an American flag. *That's* the quality of freedom that sets America apart from countless nations throughout history who have claimed to be free. In my mind that's the quality of freedom many of you fought so bravely for, even if you never imagined the use that a few spiteful people would make of it.

There's one more dimension to this issue that deserves some thought. It has to do with the impact of flag burning and other kinds of unusually ugly expression on public opinion and discourse. There may be some who believe that flag burning has the power to poison our feelings about patriotism or about America itself. I want to think about that with you. Does flag burning ever cause more people to hate the flag, or the country or way of life it represents? Is there anyone who's ever watched a flag burn, in person or on television, and said "I haven't actually thought about it before, but now that I do, the flag really is loathsome, and from now on I reject it and what it stands for?"

No. If you listen to conversations about any of the rare flag burnings that take place I think you'll find reactions go in exactly the opposite direction. In my experience a flag burner convinces people that flag burning is wrong *much more powerfully* than any speech in Congress or pamphlet from your organization ever could. It also causes some Americans to reflect on their liberty, and the gifts that war veterans have given them, with more attention than they did before. Flag burning does nothing but leave flag burners in the isolation their hatefulness deserves.

This is very much like the forces at work when there's a debate over whether groups of Nazis or other white supremacists should be allowed permits to hold demonstrations or parades, especially in minority neighborhoods. Of course they should, for the same two reasons we've been talking about: because we're strong enough in America to allow the airing of obnoxious opinions, and because Nazis on parade are the best advertisement for what's wrong with Naziism.

Some might say that's all fine for adults, but what about young children? What are they supposed to make of the sight of a burning flag? I think that's a fair question. I would answer it not with statistics or scientific surveys, but from my own experience as a parent. As I raised my children I found that they weren't very impressed by my well-meaning lectures about respect and dignity and the other values I wanted them to learn. What really left a mark were conversations triggered by dramatic, sometimes upsetting events that I didn't plan. Those were the moments that opened their minds and hearts. Those were the break-through moments of understanding that made the biggest difference.

That's not to say that witnessing dramatic events will always lead children to the conclusions we want them to draw, especially if there's no parent or caring adult around. But here's something I learned loud and clear as a parent: you're not likely to teach children that something is wrong or contemptible merely by banning it. In fact, if you want to arouse their curiosity and their appetite for trying something out, banning it may be exactly the way to go. That's how I was as child, and that's what I found with my children. Your experience may have been different, but this much I'll say with no ifs-ands-or-buts: criminalizing the burning of the flag will not increase our children's respect for it, or for the American way of life.

I will leave today understanding that many of you still disagree with me, some of you quite strongly. The plain fact is that this issue is one that divides honest patriotic Americans. That moves me to thank you yet one more time for what you've done to defend our right to disagree, sometimes with passion and even anger.

I don't want to close without offering some apology for the actions of the tiny set of people who burn flags, because I have something in common with them: I agree with some of the criticisms of government policy they have used to excuse their behavior. I am sorry that these few people would so deeply dishonor you. I suspect that if I were in your shoes I'd be gravely offended. I'd have a few choice things to say about flag burning and flag burners, and I might want to go further. I might be tempted to pull out the matchbook myself and burn some symbol that they cherish.

For *all* of that, and in the name of this country's foundational values, please resist with me the mighty urge to turn anyone's expression into a crime, so long as it doesn't threaten public safety or private property. If we start down that road, we turn America into a different nation — a nation that is not the one you and your fallen comrades fought for with devotion and courage.

Thank you very much.

★ ★ ★ ★ ★

The discussion guide for this speech is on page 138.

Six

The Two Most Powerful Words in America

Telling the U.S. Chamber of Commerce
We Need a National Health Care System

Thank you for asking me to share my thoughts about health care with you. I want to talk to you today as practical people who want to see health care work well in America and are as tired as I am of slogans and dogma and knee-jerk ideologies. I don't care if you're a fan or a dedicated critic of government programs. It's time to get this conversation focused on what works instead of abstract and threadbare philosophies.

One of the least debatable things President Bill Clinton ever said was that health care was America's great challenge. In part that's a very obvious statement, since an adequate quality of life isn't possible without physical and mental health. But there's much more than that. The failures of health care are eating away at our major social institutions and setting high hurdles on the road to a prosperous economy with robust job growth. The costs of illness and inadequate care show up in lost productivity, personal bankruptcies, increased crime, threats to classroom education and family stability. And at a time when your organization is focused on the ability of both small and large enterprises to keep overhead costs down so that they can compete in a global marketplace, health care costs have become the marauding 800 pound gorilla. I don't have to describe this burden to you. I'll bet that everyone in this room can name businesses in your communities that have sunk beneath the weight of health care costs.

We've known all this for years. With all the ingenuity and determination Americans can bring to bear on tough problems, you'd think we would have made progress towards a solution by now. We have not.

Why not? One reason is the power of two simple words. You could call them the two most powerful words in America. The first is "socialized." The second is "medicine." What does "socialized medicine" mean? I don't think I can tell you. Ask those who brandish the term around like a mighty sword and they'll say it's some kind of scheme where the government's taken over the medical system and ruined everything, like government always does. But the vagueness doesn't seem to make these two words any less powerful. They have smothered conversation and stopped new initiatives dead in their tracks. I'm here to say it's time to get over it.

To explain why I think these are the two most powerful words in America I have to nudge us to remember some facts about health care. The first is that we're spending more money on health care per person than any other country in the world. Not a *bit* more money than other countries— a *lot* more. The most reliable recent data puts per capita health spending in the United States at almost $4400 a year. The next most expensive country is Switzerland at a little under $2900 per year, followed by Canada and Luxembourg at around $2500, Germany and the Netherlands at $2300, France and Australia at about $2100, and England at about $1600 per year.[1]

---

1. *Health Affairs* Magazine (Vol 21, number 3, May/June 2002).

When you're spending more than half again as much as the second most expensive country, and more than twice as much as most of the world's affluent nations, you're probably going to want top-notch results, aren't you? You've paid for them. I'm afraid a different picture emerges from data collected by the Organization for Economic Development and Cooperation, which compares health care results from the world's most affluent countries.

OEDC figures show that the United States ranks *twenty-fourth* in average life expectancy.[2] Our infant mortality rate is among the very highest of any industrialized country.[3] After pulling together a wide variety of statistics measuring basic health standards around the world, the World Health Organization found that the United States ranks thirty-seventh among nations in what it calls "Health System Overall Performance.[4] *Thirty-seventh.*

You are businessmen and businesswomen. Would you please raise your hand if you find this situation acceptable? [pause].

Would any of you put up with this kind of gap in your own business between investment and results? [pause].

Good. You agree with a lot of committed people who are trying to create something better. Health care systems in countries that are much like ours have been carefully studied, millions of Americans have been interviewed or surveyed and a few programmatic blueprints have been hammered out and proposed. These proposals assign an important role to government — not a

---

2. World Health Organization press release, "WHO Issues New Healthy Life Expectancy Rankings," June 4, 2000.

3. "Preventing Infant Mortality: HHS Fact Sheet, U.S. Department of Health and Human Services, April 21, 2001.

4. "The U.S. Health Care System: Best in the World, or Just the Most Expensive?" http://dll.umaine. edu/ble/U.S.%20HCweb.pdf, page 4 of 8

more expensive role than government plays today, but a clearer, more visible and perhaps more active role that would reduce some of today's private sector activity. Whenever one of these proposals rises to a certain threshold level of public attention, we are rock-solid guaranteed to hear the magic words: "but — that's — *socialized medicine*." And as a practical and political matter, that ends the conversation. We can't adopt *socialized medicine* in this country. It often seems as if we can't seriously discuss any proposal, or pause long enough to ask about its details, if someone somewhere has called it socialized medicine.

What power! As things stand today, rather than exploring alternatives that someone might call socialized medicine we prefer to stick with a system that costs dramatically more money than any other in the world and yields us mediocre-to-lousy results. I'm not going to tell you that there are no downsides when government steps up to take a bigger role. But it would be nice to be able to carefully consider what they might be, and how they compare to today's downsides, wouldn't you agree? We've given these two words the power to cut off that discussion.

They don't even have to be said out loud. Sometimes they're just implied. Think back to the last time a major health care overhaul was put on the table in the early 1990s when a very famous married couple dominated the debate. Everyone in America knew their names. I don't mean Bill and Hillary Clinton. I mean Harry and Louise. They were more powerful in that struggle than anyone else. They were also fictitious, and so were the words coming out of their mouth. Without the slightest explanation of anything that was actually in the proposal, Harry and Louise convinced America that it was a bad deal. We crumpled it up and threw it away before we knew what it was.

What did we learn from the way these two carefully-cast actors brought health care reform to a screeching halt without thoughtful discussion or debate? Some would say we learned that the American people are stupid. I don't buy that. It's true that most Americans haven't let themselves think about major health care reform long enough to judge the truth and value of what Harry and Louise were saying, but that's not because they're stupid. I've had too many enlivened conversations with too many Americans to believe that.

I think it's about fear. I believe there's a zone in our minds that we've set off limits. We paper over that part of the brain with posters of myths and stereotypes. Some of those myths come straight from our memories of the old Soviet Empire, bleak gray images where hunched-over people clustered like cattle to wait for some pathetic handout or another. Years after the Berlin Wall came down this image is still so easy to invoke. You'll hear something like

"Sooo . . . seems the liberals are at it again, wanting government to take over private businesses. Well, the Soviet Union proved how well *that* works, didn't it? They proved it so well they're now on the ash heap of history, where they belong. But now some seem eager to raise them from the dead with *socialized medicine.* Just to show how stupid they think we are, they're not even bothering to change the name, did you notice that? *Socialized* medicine — the U.S.S.R., Union of Soviet *Socialist* Republics — what more do we have to know?"

You can be skeptical of new government programs, I know, without going quite that far. For millions of Americans, "government-run" has become a synonym for "shoddy," "inefficient," "bloated with waste," "unaccountable." It's the grist for endless jokes. We're asked by people who are hostile to government how we'd like this business or that to be run like the post office. Usually we agree that would be a bad idea without even thinking about it.

Well, maybe we ought to think about it. The U.S. Postal Service delivers 650 million pieces of mail each day. If you want one of those pieces to reach someone in the United States in the next couple of days, it will cost you 37 cents. They don't do it perfectly. I can tell you a couple of instances when it didn't happen like that for me. Off-hand I can't tell you about the times they got it right, which happens ten or twenty times more frequently, because when it happens correctly it doesn't stick in my mind. Do they deliver this volume of mail less reliably or more expensively than a private, profit-driven carrier like Federal Express would? Our mythology about the post office says yes, of course. Is that what well-researched facts would say?

I'm not arguing that government runs like a Swiss watch. There are plenty of changes needed, especially in the enormous federal bureaucracies. I am arguing that when with almost no real thought we say "Oh, the Postal Service, we sure don't want anything else run like the *Postal Service*," we padlock our brains at the moment we really need them. Does the U.S. Postal Service operate at a level of efficiency that we can accept in a national health care system? I'm not sure. But let's not cripple ourselves by drawing conclusions from the stand-up routines of Jay Leno and David Letterman. And if it's efficiency we want to focus on, I'll happily take the Postal Service over what passes for our health care system today. It isn't the Postal Service that spends twice as much per capita as other advanced countries while delivering consistently inferior service.

"Inferior service?" say some of the system's defenders. "Really? Is that why people from all over the world, including our neighbor to the north with the health care system that's supposed to be so great, come to the United States for highly sophisticated surgeries and other therapies? They must be suffering from some mass delusion that America provides excellent health care service, in fact the best in the world. Why else would they come here?"

Here's some confusion that we need to cut through. Politicians and medical industry executives are right when they call American health care the best in the world — in one specific, not very broad way. When it comes to the cutting edge of specialized diagnosis and treatment, the high-technology "miracles" pushing the limit of what medical science can accomplish, American medicine is the finest in the world. That's no small thing if you happen to be in critical need of those procedures. And it's a good reason for Canadians or anyone else to come here for medical care.

Somewhere along the line that fact expands into this hellish specter of a wave of Canadian humanity pouring across our northern borders for decent health care. You might want to talk to a few Canadians before you buy that story. It turns out to have the same kind of factual substance behind it as Harry and Louise's conversations.

There's a reason that I've steered my remarks towards Canada. Canada is similar to our country in most of the ways that are relevant to health care. Their system, as I'm sure you know, is called single-payer. You hear it discussed on the fringe of our political races, but not at the center. Until today you have never heard a candidate with a strong chance to win the presidency talk favorably about single-payer health insurance. That's not because most candidates think it's a bad idea. It's because whenever we come close to the outskirts of a serious discussion of single-payer health care, someone — very likely someone who works for or accepts campaign money from the prevailing health care industries — will utter the two lethal words.

If people don't run screaming from the room and instead stay to listen, they discover that single-payer isn't "socialized medicine" at all. Doctors, nurses, various therapists can be wholly private providers, and hospitals and clinics, as in our country, may or may not be privately owned. Patients are mostly free to choose their own providers, which can spur the kind of competition that improves quality and efficiency.

But I won't dispute the point if someone chooses to call the Canadian system "socialized *insurance*." It's known as single-payer because payment to the providers for health services comes from the single-source of either state or national government. I don't really care what label gets used — you can call it "Satan's Shake-Down Scheme" if you like. What I care about, and what I want you to care about, is that establishing a single insurer with a single set of standards, guidelines, payment schedules and rate cards has slashed administrative costs wherever it's been tried.

Those paper-shuffling costs account for somewhere between one-fourth and one-third of America's total health care costs.[5] That staggering figure comes into focus when you see those squads of clerical workers packed into cubicles behind the counter when you visit your doctor or medical clinic. Next time ask your doctor what they're doing. What they're mostly doing is filling out claims forms to dozens of different insurance

---

5. *New England Journal of Medicine* 336:769–774, March 13, 1997

companies with dozens of different protocols and requirements, often for the second or third time as the companies keep bouncing forms back to them to clarify the discrepancy between the summary description on line Roman numeral two, b-3 and the support data reported in the Appendix of Supplementary Form J-29, line Roman numeral four, c-2. Talk to some of the people who do this for forty hours a week. Most of them are women, probably because the job would turn some men into ax-murderers.

This is a major reason that our health system is so much more expensive than anyone else's. *It does not serve us* — not as patients, as health care providers, as tax-payers and citizens. An argument could be made that an impossibly complicated claims process may result in fewer pay-outs and serves the profit margins of the health insurance industry. But I'm not running for President in order to serve the health insurance industry.

Those who I *am* asking to serve, the people and health-consumers of America, would be the big winners with this change. We are talking about freeing up hundreds of billions of dollars for other parts of the health care system. But where there are winners — and when you're excited by a new model, it's tempting to underplay this part — there will be losers. Let's be honest about who that will be.

They won't be the basic health care providers. Reimbursement rates will be set for most procedures, just as they are in the current system, and retaining full patient choice should mean that doctors, nurses and hospitals who offer quality service will thrive. There could be impacts on the incomes of specialists at the top of the income ladder, but there are some design features that could deal with that, including private supplementary insurance to cover procedures beyond the foundation of medically necessary services.

How about the pharmaceutical industry? Well, that opens a bigger can than we can dip into today. I don't expect much enthusiasm from that sector for single-payer, because the reimbursement system will probably standardize the pay-out for medications more extensively than today's system does. Just as there is in Canada today, there will still be ample room for a good return on investment, and yes, that does include the cost of researching drugs that don't pan out. But the system I'm talking about, a system that is designed first and foremost for health consumers, will not have room to pay a drug company $20 for a pill that cost a dollar to produce and sell.

That brings us to the health insurance industry itself. I won't sugar coat this. Private health insurance is the sector that loses. If you're an executive or a major shareholder in health insurance, you probably want to find someone other than me to vote for. In the short run, what I'm proposing will be hazardous to your career or pocketbook. If you like, I could offer pithy wisdom from the human potential seminars, something along the lines of "every problem is just an opportunity in work clothes." In fact there may be room for some of you. A single-payer system could include government contracts with private vendors for insurance services, but probably not enough to accommodate all the people working in the industry today. The truth is that I don't believe America can have both a high-quality health care system and a health insurance industry as it presently exists. If anyone wants to argue the point and show me how we *can* have both, I'll listen carefully. But you'd better have something to point to that's very different from the current system.

I don't see the single-payer system as a silver bullet for trouble-free, flawlessly delivered health care. I don't believe there is a silver bullet or ever will be. What I've briefly laid out here needs extensive design work that learns from the achievements and mistakes of the Canadian experience. It's a task that should draw heavily on public input and a variety of disciplines. My hope is that some of you might consider contributing your expertise from the world of business.

Without starting to plough through the details, I want to mention three characteristics that we must build into any national health care system. You can't readily find them in what we have today. They may be easier to incorporate in a single-payer system, but not without careful and conscious design. The three are individual responsibility, *intentional* rationing of resources, and a stronger focus on the "health" in health care.

I believe we're on a fool's errand if we try to develop any system that doesn't demand personal responsibility. Health care delivery will be cost-efficient over time only if patients, you and I, stay alert and focused on what services are costing, and we will reliably be alert and focused if we're directly paying some of the cost. That will take some form of co-payment requirement, scaled to the patient's financial abilities. Otherwise we have exactly what happens when you take your car to the body shop to remove a couple dings it picked up in a crowded parking lot. When you go to retrieve it and sign the paperwork you notice the charge was $1800. "Whatever;" after all, you're not paying for it. (Once we solve the health care problem, maybe we'll be ready to tackle auto body work.)

The second thing we need is a mature grownup's recognition that a health care system is a system of choices. A health care system *rations* resources, to use another word many people don't like. Anyone who says they want a system that doesn't ration health care is asking for something that has never been and never will be. The real question is whether the rationing will be conscious or unconscious, intentional or chaotic. The seeming paradox that we have the most advanced modern

medicine on the planet and flunk some of the basic health service standards is a consequence of rationing decisions. The net
result of today's mix of forces, some of which have nothing to do
with free-market economics, is that we choose high-cost, tech-
nology-intensive service to keep very sick, generally older people alive a bit longer over providing basic preventative and
health-inducing services for the whole population.

Is that the right choice? We well may have different opinions
on that. In fact, I might have a different opinion when I
approach the end of my life than I do now. But what's not debatable is that when we direct our limited resources one way we're
choosing not to direct them elsewhere. That's what rationing
means, and conscious or not, we have always done it and always
will. Mature grownups know we make trade-offs in the real
world that have consequences. Voters, nervous about their family's well-being and particularly the health of their children,
frightened about the future of their own care and ultimately
their own mortality, sometimes let candidates help them forget
about trade-offs.

The last principle is the most basic of all. It's probably the
most daunting. Throughout this entire talk that, yes, is
approaching its conclusion, I've kept referring to "health care
systems." But I honestly don't believe America has one. Neither
does Canada, or any other nation I can name off the top of my
head. What we have is much more accurately described as "dis-
ease care systems." The preponderance of our medical resources
are devoted to easing pain and distress when something goes
wrong, instead of promoting a foundation of health that will
reduce those occurrences.

Disease-treatment will never be remotely as efficient and
effective as disease-prevention. That shift isn't one that massive
medical institutions, public or private, will be able to accom-

plish. It will come primarily from the lifestyle decisions we make as individuals and families. But I'd sure like to see the system we design make those choices more likely by stressing pre-natal care, nutrition, exercise and stress reduction. A smart system will include incentives for patients to get regularly scheduled wellness check-ups, and for providers to get the training they need to bring wellness towards the center of their practices.

Thank you for your careful attention to my case that single-payer health care would serve America far better than what we have today. I'm not asking you to leave here and start carrying that banner with me. I am asking you, I'm asking all of us, in recognition of the immense challenge to our future that health care poses to America, to *keep our eyes on the ball*. That future belongs to our children and their children. It's in their name that I ask you to stand up against fear tactics and never again let yourself be bullied by a derisive slogan, or by the counterfeit sincerity of the next Harry and Louise, into believing we can't have something better.

Please. Please don't let it be said of us that two vague words left over from the Cold War, and knee-jerk agreement with the scorn heaped on government services, kept us from giving our children the best health care system we possibly could.

Thank you very much.

★ ★ ★ ★ ★

The discussion guide for this speech is on page 139.

Seven

Stripping the Nation for Parts

Telling the Iowa Farm Council
Government Shouldn't Subsidize Ethanol

Thank you all very much for that warm welcome. I needed it tonight. I used to wonder why the first presidential primary is held in your state. Now, as a candidate working his way through the snow drifts and the hard frosts of early morning, I know: it's to figure out who really, truly wants this job.

I do. And those of us who want to be President stand here every fourth January to praise the state of Iowa and its enterprise and can-do spirit and hospitality. And that doesn't require us to stretch the truth. This is a remarkable place, not least because of the sincere and serious attention you give to politics. You seem to understand your responsibility as the first decision-makers in presidential races, and you fulfill it with a respect for the election process.

I almost said "reverence" for the process, but that would cross the line into the realm of strategic flattery, compliments that are designed to make you warm and fuzzy rather than thoughtful about the things that matter in this election. Strategic flattery is one of the tools of contemporary politics that has created the short-sighted mess we're in. So if you don't mind I'll stick with "respect" rather than "reverence" for the process, thank you sincerely for bringing to your citizen roles the kind of diligence that a quality democracy needs, and move on to speak directly to a subject that deserves our time today more than another love sonnet to Iowa from another politician looking for votes.

I've come to talk about ethanol. Ethanol is grain-based alcohol. I have a wild hunch that as Iowa's agricultural leaders you know that already. In fact I probably know less about ethanol than almost everyone in this room and I won't make the mistake of pretending otherwise. To be honest, I knew almost nothing at all about it until I decided to run for President a few months ago. And at that point the very first thing I learned about ethanol, the *only* thing I knew at the time about ethanol, was this: I am for it. I am *for ethanol.* I learned that from the consultants I brought in to help me create this campaign. They informed me that I am *for ethanol* for a very exact set of reasons.

Reason Number 1: In order to be elected President, I first have to win my party's nomination.

Reason Number 2: One key step to winning the nomination is to win or come close to winning the Iowa caucuses. The national media treats presidential politics like nothing so much as a long day at the races, and they've been waiting for endless months to announce Winners and Losers. No matter what has happened up until now, do well in Iowa and you are a Grade-A official contender. That, I'm sure you know, is why your state is so pivotal. And that's why we candidates fly thousands of miles dozens of times to walk through your beautiful snow and experience your fresh bracing weather to tell you again and again in meeting halls like this one how wonderful you and your state are. I can honestly say that you *are* wonderful, but so are a lot of states and people who never hear us tell them that. Because they're not Iowa.

Reason Number 3 that I'm *for ethanol:* Iowa produces about 440 million gallons of ethanol annually from 175 million bushels of corn each year. That's about eight percent of your state's corn crop, which means more demand for your corn and better prices for farmers. Estimates are that Iowa's ethanol industry creates 2,550 direct jobs and nearly 10,700 indirect jobs in related industry and services.[1] These are facts that translate into quality lives for some of your friends, families and neighbors. I'm going to guess these facts have at least some economic importance for everyone in this room.

Which leads straight to Reason Number Four that I'm *for ethanol*: A candidate who isn't for ethanol is not going to win the Iowa caucuses, and probably won't finish second, third or even fourth.

Those four lessons were the full textbook on ethanol provided to me by people whose job it is to get me elected. From there I decided to learn more. Not enough to become any kind of ethanol expert, but I did pick up a few more facts. Some cooled my enthusiasm a little, such as discovering that ethanol evaporates more rapidly than most other fuels, which tends to increase ozone pollution.[2] But every energy source has some drawbacks, and that one didn't seem to cut to the center of this issue.

But there's another matter that does, and it needs the attention of anyone who wants America to achieve energy independence. The short-hand term here is "net energy value." While research findings are mixed, and scientists aren't completely lined up in agreement, the best evidence I've seen says that *it takes more energy to make a gallon of ethanol than the energy a gallon of ethanol*

1. Http://www.nwicc.cc.ia.us/Module3.htm
2. President of Chevron Products Company Patricia A. Woertz, to the World Fuels Conference in 1999

provides. Studies at Cornell University's School of Agriculture find that when you add up the energy costs of corn production and its conversion into ethanol, it takes 131,000 BTUs to make one gallon of ethanol, which can provide 77,000 BTUs of energy. Every time you make one gallon of ethanol, there is a net energy loss of 54,000 BTUs. Put another way, 70 percent more energy is required to produce ethanol than the energy that ethanol generates.[3]

I'm not a farmer, I'm not a chemist and I'm not a PhD economist. But I can grasp the concept that we won't achieve energy independence and a sustainable American economy by burning nine jars of fuel to produce five. And maybe those numbers aren't exactly right; this kind of scientific analysis has a lot of variables and uncertainties to it. But without a solid, objectively-produced set of data that flips this equation around, no honest person, no one committed to treating you like grownups, can stand up and tell you this is a good energy deal for America.

One of my commitments to you is to be as consistent as I can in this campaign, to say what I believe about America to every group and audience who will listen. And it happens that this same point about net energy value came up a few days ago when I spoke to an environmental group that believes the answer to our vehicle fuel challenge is hydrogen fuel cells. Just as with ethanol, it's not hard to get excited about the concept of a clean, limitless fuel source that can power our vehicles without harming the atmosphere. And just as with ethanol, hydrogen takes more energy to produce right now than it can generate. And just as I have with you today, I told the environmental audience that we have to clear that hurdle of net energy loss before we can invest full-bore in their fuel of choice. And just as there is right

---

3. Cornell Professor David Pimental, http://healthandenergy.com/ethanol.htm

now, there were people in the room who were not happy with what I had to say.

So let me say to you, as I did to them, that the problems with your favorite fuel are not carved in stone. Ethanol and hydrogen are net energy losers today mostly because of the cost of the electric power it takes to refine them. What, then, if electric power were much cheaper? And what if in addition power could be generated without the emissions that have been changing the global climate at a life-threatening rate? And what if in addition to *that*, it could be generated in most towns and neighborhoods — sometimes on the roofs of individual *homes* — so that our highly centralized power grid, which is so vulnerable to intentional malicious attack and unintentional chain-reaction system failures, was a thing of the past?

Well, those what-ifs have some wonderful answers. One of them is that the cost of the electric power it takes to refine promising vehicle fuels like ethanol and hydrogen will steadily drop until the net energy equation I keep mentioning flips over to *positive* numbers. That's when candidates who treat voters like grownups might be able to stand up and promise major government support for the ethanol industry.

To reach that point a responsible national energy program will direct big dollars into developing the kind of power system I've just described. That means, in my judgment, a primary focus on wind and solar technologies. Anyone who still believes those sources can't be cost-effectively harnessed simply isn't paying attention to what's happening as we speak in nations across the world that, unlike us, have stayed the course towards energy independence.

None of this means we should bring ethanol R&D to a screeching halt; the fact is, there's no one magic bullet for a clean, sustainable cost-effective energy system. But it does mean, in a world where leaders have to make hard choices about spending hard dollars, that first things must be put first. And the promises my opponents are making to you about ethanol don't do that. They dig us deeper into the hole we have to climb out of before ethanol can be the viable, economically responsible fuel that we all can envision.

Why are they making those promises? Why are they *for ethanol* in a way that I no longer can be? Is it because they have good data that's markedly different with what I've been sharing with you? No. Because they come up with a different sum when they add up 2+2 than I do? I don't think so. I believe it's because they want your votes. So do I. We just have different ideas of who Iowa voters are. Unlike them, I start from the premise that you're grownups.

As I'm sure you know, there's no telling how my opponent's salute to ethanol today will translate into nuts-and-bolts outcomes if any of them are elected President. Let's assume that these aren't cynical, sweet-nothing campaign promises, that my opponents are sincere about adding ethanol support to their presidential to-do list. Then let's fast-forward to that day when one of them sits down in the Oval Office to finalize an Energy Bill, laying side-by-side an array of flawed options, and realizes that one of the less flawed among them would be to abandon support for ethanol, even though that breaks a promise made way back in the winter days of Iowa. Which means that when it matters, their position on ethanol would end up the same as mine. Because I think you're grownups, I'll tell you now.

But what if my prediction is off? There's a chance that after election one of my opponents actually would enact a big ethanol subsidy. It's happened before and could again. And that would continue a stream of resources to Iowa and Iowans that is, by itself, this year and next, a good thing.

Okay. Then what's the harm? Will an annual billion-dollar ethanol subsidy that happens to be less cost-effective than other choices mortally wound the Republic? No. Not by itself it won't. But it's not by itself. When the Iowa caucuses are over — and this may not come as shocking news — you're not going to see much of my opponents and me for a while. We'll be off to New Hampshire, which all of us want to win for the same reason we want to win here. I've learned recently that tourism has become New Hampshire's biggest industry, and that most of that is automobile touring. That has some New Hampshire business leaders urging a cut in federal gasoline taxes, so that more tourists can drive all over that state. That means that I'm in the process of learning that I'm *for lower federal gasoline taxes.*

After New Hampshire we'll all be off to tell the folks in South Carolina and Missouri and New Mexico and Oklahoma and Delaware and Arizona and North Dakota what marvelous states they have. It turns out that South Carolina is home to seven major military bases, which makes it one of our most fortified states. So, while the subject doesn't often come up while we candidates are visiting Des Moines, I may as well let you know that I'm *against further military base closures*, and I'm not especially interested in looking at a ton of boring statistics and fiscal analysis of the issue.

The state of Missouri is pinning a lot of its economic hopes on riverboat gaming. Researchers are linking a rise in divorce and substance abuse to the increase in state-sponsored gambling, but as the Missouri primary gets closer, I believe I'm learning that those researchers worry too much; I'm *for riverboat gambling.* Oklahoma's primary is the same day, and its oil industry says a whole lot of jobs could be created if a couple of minor regulations could be softened here and there and we offered a little more tax help for new drilling, and I can feel myself starting to be *for* both of those. And while we're opening up the tax code, a friendlier attitude towards mortgage interest on vacation homes sure could help two winter sunbird states like New Mexico and Arizona. I'm for that. And the annual farm bill that spends your money supporting wheat, barley and oat production? Man, I'm *for* it; wheat, barley and oats are North Dakota's biggest crops.

After the polls close in North Dakota we'll be off to Michigan, Wisconsin and Washington State, and another set of states after that and yet another the following week, a steady flow between now and the nominating conventions. There are a lot more things we'd better be *for* real soon. I can't quite remember them at the moment; it could be they haven't yet told me what I'm going to be *for* a month from now, so that I won't lose focus on what I'm for this week. But if you could travel along with us for a month or two you'd be impressed by how earnestly we'll be for them.

I don't want to wallow in cynicism here; this country has had about as much cynicism as it can afford. You get the point. If we follow the tried-and-true formula for winning the quantity of votes that will make us viable candidates, my opponents and I are going to come out energetically for a whale of a lot of specific, varied, sometimes even contradictory things. Specific, varied, *expensive* things.

It's that long wobbly list, and not the single, economically debatable issue of ethanol subsidies, that's our problem here. And it's a big one. It's so big that it moves me to come before you with an urgent request. I make it for the sake of this country, and therefore for *Iowa's* sake. And it's this:

Don't ask me to make a promise here in Iowa that hands a bad deal to Americans in New Hampshire and South Carolina and Arizona, and then move on to *those* states refusing to make any promises that might hand a bad deal to Americans in Iowa. Don't ask me to protect your interests out there in the midst of powerful political temptations and forget about the best interests of other Americans as I stand here asking for your votes. If I do that, there's no way I can lift my right hand a year from now with a clear conscience and swear to serve all Americans to the best of my ability.

I know that the people of this state aren't indifferent to the well-being of people elsewhere. I also know that when times get tough and the future seems shaky — times like today — nearly anyone will grab an opportunity for short-term gains without much thought to the big picture. But here's the irony: that very grabbing, and the election-year pandering of politicians like us that encourage that grabbing are two big reasons for our tough times. Because when political leaders crisscross the country tossing promises and money around like sugary treats from a piñata, they are plundering the resources we need to build a viable future for America. And I believe that in the quiet of your own thoughts, each of you already knows that, even as you ask us to support projects that might be part of that raid. I say that with humility, because if I myself lived and worked here in Iowa I would probably be asking for exactly what you are asking us for. And I'd probably be leaving this meeting with mixed thoughts: hope that the next President will go to bat for ethanol in a big way, right next to a longing for something better, some-thing *more whole*, for America.

That better America is within our reach, but not if we give in to a politics that dismantles our country as if it were a classic car, pulling off a chromed mirror here and a shiny fender there and ripping off the hood to raid the engine compartment of any part that can be sold for votes. That will leave us, not too long from now, with the rusting hulk of a chassis. I believe the chassis has been picked over too much already. If we can keep ourselves from picking off even more, I know we can rebuild it into a finer vehicle than we had before.

And you can have a decisive role here in Iowa if you want it. As the first primary state, the state with every political eye on it at this dramatic time, you could make history by voting for the candidate who *doesn't* try to buy you over with the political goodies that the pundits say you demand. You could prove that you're committed to this country in a much broader and more thoughtful way than they expected, and when you do that you'll be inviting Americans in the other 49 states to do the same thing. That's what I would call leadership.

I'm about to visit the states I just mentioned, and I'll be saying in each of them what I've just said to you: I can't sign on for their special interest unless it lines up with the best interests of America as a whole. As I do that, do you know what would delight me more than anything else? It would be to point to this state and remind people that the pundits said that no candidate could win here without pushing ethanol. And then to be able to say *"The pundits were wrong*: the people of Iowa see what decades of bribing voters have done to America, and they want something better, something more valuable to them than a narrow short-term pay-off for Iowa. They know that the 'Greatness of America' is more than a throw-away phrase in a campaign speech, and they're going to fight for it."

Are you ready to take that on? Will you let me take that message to people across America? I'd sure be proud to carry it.

Thank you.

★ ★ ★ ★ ★

The discussion guide for this speech is on page 140.

Eight

The Camel's Damned Nose

*Telling the National Abortion Rights Action League
to Compromise With its Opponents*

Thank you. I'm glad to be with you today. I should tell you that when you run for President you have to start every speech telling your audience how glad you are to be with them, whether you mean it or not. Today I mean it. NARAL and other groups that fight for reproductive rights have stood solidly behind me since I ran for my first office, based on what I've said and on my record. I'm proud of both my record and your support. So on a long, grinding campaign trail it's exceptionally comfortable and usually fun to come speak to you.

I'm not sure how much fun we'll have today. I've come to challenge you, and to challenge myself to be honest with you. The steady ferocity of the attack on reproductive rights can make it hard to speak our minds fully to one another. Everyone in this room may be wholly committed to keeping abortion safe and legal in America, but my guess is there are different views on some important details. We should be able to talk about them in the same spirit of inquiry, respect and careful listening that you bring to most parts of your lives.

But in my experience we don't. I know why we don't. The middle of a battlefield isn't an easy place to open fully to challenging, dissonant ideas, especially when some of them come from the people who are shooting at you. And we are without question on a battlefield still, *still* defending a basic right earned over years of hard, bitter struggle.

I'm here to suggest that we open ourselves to some of those dissonant ideas. Not in order to become "better people" in some warm fuzzy way — maybe that will happen and maybe it won't — but for practical reasons. There is a decisive mass of people in America who are ambivalent or confused about this issue, and we'd better try making room for them. I believe we need them. I believe abortion rights won't be secure in this country until a larger portion of Americans understand fully what they are. That won't happen if what they get from us is rigidity and contempt.

I want to go straight to the core of this struggle, where there are two primary elements.

One is that millions of women around the world demand control over their own bodies and reproductive systems. It's outrageous that people in power want to take that control away, particularly male people in power who don't get pregnant a lot and have no clue about, and often no interest in, the reality of that experience.

The second is this: in the minds of some Americans, abortion is murder. For the moment I'm not talking about the cynical opportunists, the politicos from conservative districts who use the issue to claim moral superiority and duck the persistent economic and social problems that they should be tackling. I'm not talking about red-faced religious leaders who use it to whip their flocks into a righteous lather. I'm talking about everyday people with no way to make money or political capital off the struggle, people who are doing the best they can to understand life and how they fit into it.

More than a few of those people believe that abortion is murder. One response to that has been an unending debate on the question of when human life begins. That turns out to be a question that science can inform but can't answer. We answer that question for ourselves while the millions of people who oppose us answer it for *them*selves. There will never be a white-jacketed referee with a clipboard to settle it for us.

This unresolvable question makes abortion rights an unresolvable issue. It seems to make compromise nonsensical. We're over here insisting on a woman's right to choose. Yet along with everyone else, we understand that there are choices an individual can't be allowed to make. Rape is one. Burning down your neighbor's home is another. Murder is another. So there are people who will never concede your right to have an abortion for the same exact reason that you'd never concede their right to murder a baby. They can't compromise the point, just as you wouldn't. What you may think of that perspective doesn't change the fact that millions of Americans hold it.

And so the impasse. If you're looking at opponents who can't compromise, you're not inclined to give up any ground. Why should you? I'll try to answer that question, starting with some reflection on the range of people who don't share our commitment to reproductive freedom.

And a range is exactly what it is, stretching out to the end I just described, where people believe abortion is murder. There are millions of Americans on the spectrum between that viewpoint and ours. Many of them are the swing voters you always hear about, as in "swing them our way and we win." Their views are ambivalent or unformed, and depending on the issue they make up 15 to 70 percent of the electorate. Simple math says they'll make the difference in most elections. That includes elections where the winner gets to appoint Appeals Court and Supreme Court justices.

What's the attitude of swing voters on reproductive rights? Some of you may have polling data with crisp answers to that, but for the moment let me sketch out some broad lines. I believe there are millions of Americans who prefer staying as far away from this struggle as they can. They *don't* like the notion of terminating pregnancies. They *don't* like the notion of the government or anyone else meddling in a woman's most personal and intimate decisions. They might wonder if there's anything out there that could smooth the sharp edges of this dilemma. Can't there be a middle ground? The evangelists and self-described social conservatives say "no" with a violent dogmatism that turns off many in the middle. They might look to us. Do we have a rigid "no" for them, too, or can we offer something else?

Maybe not. Maybe we have to dig in as deep and unyielding as those who'd ban all abortions, and hope somehow we have the numbers and luck to keep five people on the Supreme Court who will defend a woman's right to choose. Maybe. But I want to explore a different way. What happens if we open more broadly to what some of those people across the middle of the spectrum have to say? What if we explore ways to smooth a couple of those sharp edges? Would that create an opening to expand our voting numbers and move judicial appointments in our direction?

Some of you are frowning now. What "sharp edges" am I talking about? Where are the patches of middle ground we can explore? There are two that keep surfacing into legislative proposals: adult notification and 24-hour waiting periods.

This brings us to where I wasn't sure if we'd have fun today. It's more fun to remember the victories we've enjoyed together and plan new ones than it is to talk about this. Many of your other friends in political office won't touch it for fear of losing your support. That can happen. You could leave today wondering how true a friend I am after all. I've always believed that a true friend sometimes says things you don't want to hear. So let me offer what's meant to be true friendship.

In recent years you have fought off parental consent laws in one state legislature after another. You've argued forcefully that requiring a minor girl to get permission from parents who oppose abortion, who are abusive in one way or another — who in some atrocious cases may even be responsible for the girl's pregnancy — is unrealistic and cruel. Thank you for that stand. Because it is so clearly right, proposals have evolved over time from parental consent to parental notification; parents don't necessarily have to approve an abortion, but they do have to know about it. You've accurately pointed out that may not be a very big improvement. It too can subject a girl to brutal, even life-threatening consequences at the hands of sick parents.

The logic of that position, too, has generally won out. So recent notification bills have dropped the requirement of involving parents at all before their daughter's abortion. A minor girl fearful of her parents could confer instead with a designated professional — usually a judge, an ordained minister, a licensed social worker or certified teacher — but she wouldn't need their consent to proceed.

I say that's a far cry from the starting place of parental consent proposals. With the right safeguards in place, I would support it. It seems reasonable to me, and it's my judgement that it seems so reasonable to the millions of Americans in the middle that they're not able to understand or respect opposition to it. I think they resonate to an argument that our opponents love to use again and again. I know you've heard it: while we routinely require parental permission for almost any health services they receive right down to stitching a minor cut, we don't for abortion. What's that about? Is this really a decision we want a terrified 13-year-old girl to make all by herself? I don't want to have to answer "yes" to that question. I don't believe the fight over adult notification is one we can win in the court of public opinion. Fighting that fight can corner us into looking as dogmatically irrational as the far-right fringe. That's not what those millions of middle Americans are looking for.

The other edge I want to mention is the proposal to require 24-hour waiting periods before all or most abortions. In their push for waiting periods, anti-choice leaders like to bring forward women who say they deeply regret their abortions. They imply that most women come to feel that way. I don't buy that, but I'm sure it happens sometimes. And that it happens at all is for some Americans a persuasive argument for waiting periods, not of weeks or days, but of twenty-four hours, one full day after a woman first comes in to see a doctor.

What's wrong with that idea? Two things. First of all it's patronizing — downright offensive, some would say — because it says that women don't really know their own minds, they can act out of impulse or hormones against their own, quote "true," endquote, best interest. I hear the insult in that message and won't tell you to pretend it's not there.

The other problem with a waiting period requirement is practical. When the debate comes up we're told that a 24-hour waiting period could drop an insupportable burden on low-income women who come to town from rural homes and would need motel rooms they can't afford. Well, as a man with some money, I've never been in that position. I'm sure it could happen. But as I listen carefully to that argument, as I listen for the music behind the words, my gut says *Come on, that's not the heart of this matter.* The unaffordable motel bill and even the

patronizing message are not what ignites activists to fight wait-
ing-period bills with all their might. And my sense is the same
about adult notification; what is centrally at stake is not the lit-
eral question of whether we should require a child to talk to a
skilled professional adult before she has an abortion. I realize
that some of you don't like either idea on the merits. At the same
time I believe something is moving you more deeply than the
merits, or demerits, of these two proposals.

I believe what really fuels your opposition to these proposals is the dreaded nose of the camel. Adult notification and 24-
hour waiting periods may or may not be reasonable, but if
they're accepted then the camel's nose is in the tent. His head,
neck, shoulders won't be far behind. You believe, correctly I
think, that some anti-choice leaders are fighting for waiting periods and notification as the first steps to achieve the real agenda
of banning abortion entirely.

The "real agenda." That's become one of politics' top-ten
phrases, with plenty of inflection on the *REAL*. You hear it
applied to gays, environmentalists, trade unions and gun control
activists. "Those gays may say they only want marriage licenses,
but their *real* agenda..." and then you can fill in the blank.
"Those enviros *say* they just want trees protected close to the
creeks, but their *real* agenda..." Dot-dot-dot. "That Brady
Bunch, all they're talking about now is gun-show background
checks and trigger locks, but that's not their *real* agenda."

I'm not here to ridicule that fear. It's worth thinking about,
because in all these cases covertly advancing a larger "real agenda" is exactly what some people have in mind. That calls for
healthy skepticism and vigilance. But does it mean we don't
even consider exploring the middle ground, or looking for
bearable concessions that might meet more needs than we're
meeting now? Who gave extremists with covert agendas the

power to veto good-faith attempts to narrow the gaps between us? All of us who are too scared of the camel's damned nose to open our ears, that's who.

The camel's nose theory assumes a weakness that we may not have. It implies that the tent is made of some delicate fabric that will collapse as the camel moves in. That may be home for some people, but it's not ours. Our structure is steady and firm. This camel is nosing around the foundation of a concrete bunker, not a tent flap. What I'm suggesting is a shift from "We will never give you an inch" to "We have a fundamental principle that we will never violate: the only one who has authority over a woman's body and reproductive function is that woman herself. If within that framework you have a concern we might be able to meet, let's talk about it." And that framework, that concrete foundation, need never change.

Do some of you who've fought in the trenches all these years find that naive? I can't blame you for that. What happens when you give an inch to people who never will? It might encourage them, it's true. They could tell themselves that our concessions on these two issues, after years of holding fast, mean we'll yield even more. We would soon show them they're wrong about that, no matter how hard they keep shoving on the camel's rear end.

I'm more interested what the effect could be on those millions of swing voters. It might be that many would welcome what they'd see as a breakthrough of common sense and humane accommodation in what's been a deadlocked war of dogma. And that could be what's been missing for them as they've looked for their place in this struggle. We need more of their votes than we've had until now, and I think we can have them.

"Could" be. "Might" be. Can I prove of any of this? Of course not. What's clear to me, though, is that abortion rights in America survive by a thread that is thinner than it needs to be in a nation of people that are more tolerant than their voting records show. I believe we can do something about that if we focus our commitment to reproductive freedom so clearly and cleanly that we're able to listen compassionately to those who don't fully agree with us. Sometimes a camel's nose is just a nose.

You've listened to me today when you don't wholly agree with me. I'm grateful for that, and for your tenacious and immensely important work over the years.

Thank you.

The discussion guide for this speech is on page 141.

Nine

The Definition of Insanity, Illustrated

Telling the Anti-Drug Coalition of America
to Move Towards Legalization

Thanks very much for the opportunity to join you today. The first thing that came to mind after I received your invitation to speak to the issue of national drug policy was an old definition of "insanity" that Bill Clinton made popular when he was president You remember it, don't you?

Insanity is doing the same thing over and over again and expecting different results.

With that definition you can make a good case that insanity abounds in today's world, so much so that picking one single public policy as more insane than the others is a challenge. But if you forced me to do that, I'd have to go with the War on Drugs.

The War on Drugs has been pursued since I was in college, and that's a long time ago. How has it fared? We don't have to guess about that. A mountain of statistical information collected over the years answers the question. I want to spend a minute scanning some of it with you.

In 1973, we arrested 328,000 people in this country for drug crimes. Roughly 1.6 million, almost five times as many, were arrested for drugs in 2001, almost half of those for possession of

marijuana. As you'd expect, our investment in dollars follows
those numbers. Federal spending for the War on Drugs went
from $1.65 billion in 1982 to just under $20 billion in 2003,
more than a twelve-fold increase. And by 1999, more than half
of our high school students had tried illegal drugs before gradu-
ating. In that year a widely circulated survey called "Monitoring
the Future" reported that 41 percent of American tenth-graders
had tried pot, while the average figure in Western Europe, which
uses treatment and education much more than punishment, is
17 percent.[1]

Our state governments, according to a 2001 Columbia
University Study, are spending about 77 percent of their combined budget for courts, prisons, prosecutors and jails on drug-
related cases. And since mandatory minimum sentencing for
drug users began in 1986, the Federal Bureau of Prisons budget
has increased by over 2000 percent, from $220 million to about
four and a half billion dollars. The Justice Department's Bureau
of Justice Statistics says 80% of the population increase in federal prisons from 1985 to 1995 came from drug convictions.[2]

After that kind of spending, the people who foot the bill —
you and me — might be excused for expecting some serious
progress. One reason we're not getting it comes from a study by
United Nations Office for Drug Control and Crime Prevention.
They found that profits in illegal drugs are so inflated that you'd
have to intercept three-quarters of all drug shipments before you
took away enough profit to shut them down. That's 75 percent.
Yet after the twenty-fold budget increases I've described, the
highest estimates say that 13 percent of heroin shipments and

---

1. Common Sense for Drug Policy 2004 *Factbook*
   (www.drugwarfacts.org/factbook.pdf) item #2, p 4; and #22, p 9.
2. Ibid, #21, p 54; #30, p 158; and #3, p 154.

perhaps one-third of cocaine shipments are being intercepted.[3]

A recent Rand Corporation study found that we can reduce the societal costs of drugs by $7.50 by investing either *one* dollar in abuse treatment programs, or *fifteen* dollars in additional law enforcement, prosecution and prison spending. Put another way, the War on Drugs costs us fifteen times more than treatment programs to get the same improvement. Yet more than two-thirds of the nineteen billion federal dollars we spent in 2002 went for police, prosecutors and prisons while less than one-third went to treatment and education. States spent about $24 billion all together prosecuting and punishing drug offenders while spending $513 million, or about *three percent as much*, on treatment and prevention.[4]

Over 80 percent of the increased number of federal prisoners from 1985 to 1995 were from drug convictions, the vast majority of which were non-violent. Now, put that together with one more statistic from the same source: *one-quarter of the people who are first put in federal prisons for non-violent offenses go back a second time for violent crimes.*[5] Think about the kind of nation we become with that trend at work for another decade or two.

With much of this in mind, one authority whose name you know said this to an annual conference of the National Institute on Drug Abuse: "I believe that we have created an American gulag." Those were the words of General Barry McCaffrey, who at the time served as America's top drug enforcement officer under President Clinton.[6] [pause]

---

3. Ibid, #3, p 50.
4. Ibid, #s 30–31, p 56; #11, p 51; and #s 23–24, p 54.
5. Ibid, #3, p 154; and #22, p 157.
6. Ibid, #26, p 158.

Is that enough? I could rattle on and on for the rest of the day and the picture wouldn't change. What we have here is thirty years of on-the-ground results so relentlessly clear that we don't have to spend ten seconds debating whether we're winning this war. We are not. We've been completely overrun, sacked and pillaged. Blowing the trumpet for another multi-billion charge up the hill is, in a perfect example of the definition we're using, *insane*.

Yet charge again we will. Why? We should be posing that question to politicians who keep waging the War on Drugs. Ask them why, with over three decades of results this consistent and this grim, they want to keep doing the same thing. (You could ask them "What have you been *smoking?*" but don't expect a smile; with results this terrible, there's really not a lot to laugh about.)

What they will tell you in response is that illegal drugs are a scourge that does horrible things to people, especially our children. They'll be hoping that somehow you'll take that as an answer to your question. It is not. I hope you'll ask them again. You could say, yes, I understand that part, I understand how bad these drugs are, but that wasn't my question. My question is why you keep sticking to a strategy that has been so expensive and so stunningly unsuccessful, year after year after year, in dealing with these bad drugs?

What you will probably hear then is a second declaration of how bad drugs are, maybe with some different phrasing. You can actually go three or four rounds like this with some people. They'll keep saying drugs are bad and you keep saying yes, I know, so why do you keep doing things again and again that don't reduce their use? Be persistent. You're not likely to get a good answer, but if enough people keep asking the same question long enough, it might start to dawn on political leaders that there's a difference between passionate, table-pounding anti-drug speeches and effective drug policies, and that their voters have figured out that difference — that voters, finally, are demanding straight talk.

Instead of straight talk, the conversations we have about drugs, especially during campaign season, usually begin with a kind of loyalty oath. No matter where a political speech on the subject ends up, it has to start with references to the "dark horrors" or the "domestic Holocaust" of illegal drug use. If you don't start there, you find yourself adrift in very hazardous seas. This much I know: we politicians are not likely to provide any worthwhile leadership on drugs when we can't even talk about them with a straight face.

What gets in our way here? What makes otherwise decent leaders so tongue-tied, so afraid that they might let a full paragraph go by without a denunciation of drugs? I have one answer to that, and it has its seed in a very wholesome impulse. I think politicians trip over themselves to establish anti-drug credentials because they understand our intense and genuine concern for youngsters, especially the particular ones we love. The thought of drugs crippling or killing them is almost more than we can bear. So from the standpoint of someone looking for votes, *it becomes much more important to be absolutely clear that you're against drugs than it does to surface ideas that might actually do something about them.* And if we come to this issue during campaigns with the overriding goal of swearing our opposition to drugs more forcefully than the other guys, we're not inclined to say anything at all that might confuse the matter.

With all of us who want to be President climbing over each other to prove we're the *most* opposed to drugs, no wonder our government keeps "doing the same thing over and over again and expecting different results." We're stuck here with our eyes closed and fingers crossed, hoping, just *hoping* that eventually these laws and punishments will somehow succeed. *Please*, just let them succeed.

This is a tragedy. It is a tragedy exactly because drugs *are* doing so much violence to so many Americans. Heroin and crack cocaine have devastated our inner cities and ravaged a generation of young people, most of them black and brown. Methamphetamine has killed more people in this country than we can know, and burned out the insides of many more. Marijuana's a more debatable substance — and please let's be clear that telling our smart, observant youngsters that marijuana is just as damaging as heroin isn't helping anyone — but there's nothing pretty about the dulling and befuddling impact it has on youngsters who are trying to get traction in their lives.

Those are the politically easy things to say about drugs. They are also *exactly the reason* we have a solemn duty to stop posturing about drugs. We have a duty to stop pretending that the length of prison sentences that we mandate somehow correlates with how concerned and determined we are. We have a solemn duty to find what will work better than this pathetic failure of a war.

And let's ourselves be clear about something that's *very* clear to our youngsters: none of these drugs have killed as many people, or prematurely stripped as many of their health, as have alcohol and cigarettes, the staples of two of the most profitable and politically potent industries in America. This tough fact deserves its own discussion some other time. For now I'll just note our peculiar notion that we can effectively warn our children off dangerous drugs while clinging for dear life to tobacco, hard alcohol, and prescription medications far beyond what prudent medical care would call for, a grab-bag of legal drugs with deadlier track records than the substances we are *begging* our youngsters not to take — that we sometimes *lock them up* for taking!

When we preach about drugs against this backdrop, when we criminalize their use, what we're saying is "Do as we say, not as we do." Here's my question for those of you who have raised children: have you had a lot of success with that approach? Neither have I. We're fooling ourselves if we think we'll get far with this insanely mixed message. Insanity, remember, *is doing the same thing over and over again and expecting different results.*

I come to you ready to work as hard as it takes, and to try whatever it takes, to minimize the ravages of drug use. But if you tell me we have to fight this battle without doing anything about the advertising-fueled multi-billion dollar trade in tobacco and hard alcohol, without challenging the massive overprescription of so-called medicines to increase the profits of politically powerful industries, then I will tell you to count me out. I won't waste my time on hypocritical ventures that are sure to fail, and I hope you don't either.

But don't count anyone out yet. There are things we can do to reduce the human tragedy of drug use, and the rash of crime that surrounds it. I know that to be true because the countries of the world that are most like America are doing some of those things, with results so much better than the miserable statistics I shared with you a little earlier. "Oh, those other countries," someone might be thinking. "What, like Sweden or Denmark or the Netherlands? But do we really want to be like them? They're so *permissive*." Yes, those are three of the countries I'm thinking of, but not just those three. If you pinned a map of the world on the wall, blind-folded yourself and threw a dart, it would land on a country with better results than we've had.

And as for "permissive" — well, there's a word that leads to all kinds of juicy issues. But before we indulge in lofty moral debates about permissiveness, would it be all right if we first take some practical steps to deal with the present disaster?

What's *beyond* debate is the fact that those countries, with media and cultural influences much like ours, imprison much smaller percentages of their population, which means they're creating many fewer career criminals. Drugs kill, cripple and addict many fewer of their people. Profit-motivated crime to compete for and buy drugs — which is to say, crime that afflicts almost every American city — barely exists in many of those countries.

Those are *results*, not abstract ideas. What interests me is results. What I think should interest every politician who speaks with such heart-wrenching concern about drugs is results. The stakes are too high to get distracted by anything else.

The proven results from some of these countries mean that we don't have to start from square one to design better drug policies. We're not likely to lift their programs exactly as they are and set them down here in this country, because we're not exactly like any other country. But there is plenty to learn here, and plenty to work with. And in fact many able, passionately concerned people in this country have been working away, no matter how hostile the political environment, for a long time. A recent editorial in the *Ram*, the student newspaper at Fordham University, says it plainly and clearly. Here's what those young people have to say.

> "There is a growing movement to change these destructive and failed policies. Headed by rational-thinking public policy advocates, this movement includes the victims, and the families of the victims of the war on drugs. It also includes judges and police officers on the front-lines of this war, corrections officers who remember when prisons housed real criminals, not petty nonviolent offenders, recovering addicts who can't get

methadone from their doctors, nurses in oncology or AIDS units forced to look the other way as patients in pain smoke marijuana illegally, farmers forbidden from growing hemp, and African Americans stopped by police for 'driving (or walking) while black.' What we need is drug policy reform that includes decriminalization and redefines drug use in medical, social, and economic terms. We need a policy grounded in common sense, human rights, science and public health, not one based on prejudice, fear and ignorance and the vested pecuniary interests of law-enforcement and the prison industrial complex. We need to call an end to the War on Drugs."

Indeed we do. In order to protect our children and their children from the scourge of drugs, can we loosen our grip on our disproven theories? Can we stop doing the same ineffective things over and over again and start fighting for better results for our children? Of course we can.

Thank you very much.

★ ★ ★ ★ ★

The discussion guide for this speech is on page 142.

Ten

Just Say NO to Legislative Terrorism

Telling the National Press Club
Why Must-Pass Budget Bills Must Be Vetoed

Good afternoon, and thanks for inviting me here on what turns out to be an important day for our country's future.

Right this moment as we meet here, a Congressional bill is about to land on the President's desk for his signature. It will hit with a loud thump, because it runs several thousand pages long. This is the Omnibus Spending Bill of 200_, and it contains this year's budget for a dozen, that's *twelve* of the Departments of the United States government. It provides for the spending of about 820 billion tax dollars.

The President will definitely sign this bill. When he does he's likely to tell us that it's not perfect, but the consequences of not signing it are too great to accept. He will likely point out that it includes programs to shelter, feed and provide essential care for millions of Americans who would otherwise suffer and perhaps even die. In a moment we'll review a few other provisions of this bill that are, to put it gently, extremely hard to justify. The President won't try to justify them, nor will members of Congress when they're asked why they voted Aye. Their answer will be short and sweet. They will say "We had no choice."

And *that* . . . is not true. Here's what I want you to know: if it were me sitting down in the Oval Office desk with pen in hand, I would veto this bill. *I would veto it.* I'd also make sure to deploy short-term resources every way I could to prevent or soften the blow to vulnerable people that this veto might cause. But even knowing that those emergency measures might fall short — even if my decision would harm some Americans today — I would step up and veto this bill, because signing it would be renewing a cynical process that is doing deeper and longer-lasting harm to this country.

Before I say more about that, let's first be clear that we shouldn't be in this predicament in the first place. With a fair measure of presidential leadership and Congressional competence, a bill this bad would never make it to the Oval Office. We're in the last week of January. The budget authorized by this gargantuan bill technically went into effect *last* October 1. That timing fits a film like *Back to the Future* better than it does constitutional government, but the fact is that the President is about to approve spending that took place 15 weeks ago. With the invention of modern parliamentary miracles like Continuing Resolutions, that may be a debatable statement in technical terms, but I think anyone who's honest and knowledgeable in the ways of Washington knows what I mean.

It wasn't always like this. There actually was a time not so very long ago when Congress examined, debated and passed budgets one department at a time *before* the beginning of the fiscal year. It was never a perfect process, but it had enough deliberation and care to it that for the most part you could say that our elected representatives had a genuine role in approving the budgets that run our country.

Today the idea of timely consideration of the budget seems quaint. Congress completes its budgets later and later into the fiscal year, now close to *four months late,* and nobody seems to care much. Maybe the concept of deadlines seems a little old-fashioned and arbitrary these days. Tardiness, when you get right down to it, isn't exactly a mortal sin, is it? As long as stop-gap continuing resolutions keep funding government in the meantime, there's no serious problem here, right?

Wrong. The problem's not that this bill is so late, it's that it's so omnibus. What does that word mean, anyway? One of my dictionaries defines "omnibus" as "providing for many things at once; comprehensive; including all or everything." That's pretty clear. But there's an older definition that may convey the flavor better. An "omnibus," according to a popular online dictionary, is "a long four-wheeled carriage, having seats for many people; especially, one with seats running lengthwise, used in conveying passengers short distances." Remember that part about "short distances," please.

The problem is that no mortal human being has the capacity to pass competent judgment on a bill that has, to go back to the first definition, quote, "all or everything," endquote, of the federal budget in it. As recent weeks and months passed with final action on *none* of these big budgets, there amassed a mountain of unresolved alternatives, trade-offs, details and disputes so huge that no Congress, however skilled and honest and well-staffed it might be, can responsibly handle it. I doubt there's a member of Congress who could tell you broadly and accurately what's *in* this enormous Frankenstein of a bill. When lawmakers know very little about the money measures they're passing we have a problem.

Actually we have two problems. One is much older than anyone in this room. We call it pork, and it runs deeper than the legislative malpractice of late, massively conglomerated budget bills. There is some evidence — and please lean towards me, so that no one overhears this — indicating that on occasion

Congress spends money to advantage its members in the next election, or to pay off campaign contributors, in ways that might not serve the public interest in a big way. We've become so jaded about pork as a reality of political life that it's easy to forget that the pork in our public spending, the fat that benefits an unjustifiably small slice of America at the expense of everyone else, has huge consequences. Here are three that first come to mind.

I don't have to tell you that most of our fifty states — all of which, by the way, actually balance their budgets every year instead of pulling out the mega-Visa Card the way Washington does — are in miserable fiscal shape. Public schools are cutting out school days, packing more and more kids into fewer classes and in some cases closing. Public and mental health agencies are shutting down, police patrols are dwindling, food and housing assistance are evaporating, public colleges are zooming out of economic reach for more and more people, criminals are springing loose for lack of jail cells or legal representation. It's very grim, and it's happening just about everywhere. When governors and state legislators get together and ask the federal government for help — even when they ask the feds to deliver on their promises to fund services that Washington *requires* them to provide, services like special education in public schools — our national leaders shake their heads and make regretful little clucking sounds. "We'd love to help you out, ladies and gentlemen, really we would. But the money's just not there. How about a tote bag that says 'The White House' on it?" I submit to you that a whole lot of the money is "just not there," friends, because it was spent on pork.

Side effect number two is that pork saps our ability to change course, and I think you'll agree with me that some courses need changing. I'm talking about big changes in our health care system, in how we transport people and freight, in our energy systems, and in the breadth of economic opportunity, which speaks directly to our systems of public education. What I'm talking about won't be cheap. We can't effectively change any of these systems without transitional programs that cost real money.

Take transportation as one example. We have the industrial base in this country to produce the infrastructure and equipment for the trains and buses and other elements of a great public transit system — a system that's convenient and pleasant enough to replace the single-driver / single-car system that clearly can't go on forever. Much of that industrial base is occupied today with the manufacture of weapons systems and munitions that don't make sense today. But they do allow a few companies to stay profitable, and a lot of people to stay employed. Instead we could employ them making things we really need. That won't come about by snapping our fingers and ordering them to change over tomorrow morning. This transition, which is just one of several that could nudge America back on track, will cost money — the money, you'll remember, that's "just not there."

The third side effect is this: the torrent of pork in Washington is pumping up the stack of IOUs we're handing to our children and their children. Let's be honest with ourselves about this: unless we extinguish the spending fire that is fueled by this kind of pork, *the central condition of our children's and grandchildren's lives will be the struggle to get out of debt.* We have to decide if that's acceptable to us. If it's not, the way we've been thinking about America needs a big overhaul. Let me tell you a story.

Many years ago I made a public television documentary on a major federal dam proposed for a tributary of the Rogue River in Southern Oregon. A federal investment of about $160 million was at stake. The opponents were armed with clear bold-faced findings from the Congressional Budget Office that at *best*, the project would return about 70 cents in benefits for every dollar in costs. And no one was challenging those numbers.

The dam had plenty of supporters anyway. They were local developers, realtors, contractors, county commissioners and city councilors, and they told anyone who would listen how important it was for Southern Oregon to take advantage of this rare opportunity. I remember interviewing one of them for the documentary, an articulate real estate broker who spoke brightly to the camera about how vital the dam would be to the region's water capacity in the 21st century. When I asked him about the CBO's gloomy cost-benefit figures, he shrugged them off with a "lies, damned lies and statistics" kind of comment. I asked him if he'd be backing the dam if we in Southern Oregon had to pick up the cost ourselves. He stared at me for two seconds and said "We'll cross that bridge when we come to it."

Minutes later he came over to shake my hand as I was packing away the video camera. "You kind of got me with those cost-benefit figures," he said. "And to be truthful, this thing doesn't exactly pencil out. But I'll tell you this: we've worked hard to get those dollars lined up for us in Washington. And if we don't take them, then somebody else will, probably for a project doesn't pencil any better than ours does. We'd be suckers not to take it."

We'd be suckers not to take it. Someone should carve that phrase in stone in the Capitol rotunda. To this day I haven't heard a better summary of the inside attitude towards public spending that prevails in and around Washington. I don't believe I have to say anything about where this kind of thinking, which you can find in every Congressional district in America, will take us.

What does all of this have to do with the great big tardy Omnibus Budget Bill? After all, pork was around back even when budgets were finished on time, right? Of course. But today's process makes pork much easier to hide. With omnibus spending on this scale, pork projects become needles in haystacks the size of obsolete aircraft carriers. It's nearly impossible for the public and media to hold Congress accountable when the pork is surrounded by thousands of line-items covering every kind of government expenditure.

Now, there's a second problem that goes beyond good old-fashioned pork. It's about forcing down the throat of this country laws we *specifically* don't want. That's not my opinion. It's the opinion of the very same Congress that just passed the Omnibus Budget Bill, because when they directly considered these provisions just in the last few weeks, they said *NO, thanks, these are bad ideas.*

What bad ideas were resurrected from the Congressional trash heap and stuffed into this must-pass budget? The one that most people heard about was the reinstatement of FCC rule changes to allow major media corporations to increase their holdings past the old limitations. Those changes were angrily rejected a few weeks ago by a big bipartisan majority of Congress, but forget about that; as soon as the President signs the Omnibus Bill, the *specifically rejected* rules allowing media giants to grow will become the law of the land.

Here's another: the National Rifle Association has been fighting to force government agencies to destroy records on gun purchases after just 24 hours, instead of keeping them up to 90 days as the current law sometime allows. Congress found that proposal so drastic in today's environment that it did something very unusual: it said "no" to the NRA. With recent votes Congress said the swift destruction of those records wouldn't serve America. But that's exactly what will happen after the President signs this Omnibus Bill. That provision will become the law of the land.

And as you probably know the President wants a thorough re-working of the laws regulating overtime work in America. He says he wants to square regulation with modern workplace realities and give more American workers a fair shake. The unions that represent those workers see things differently, to put it mildly. The struggle's been raging for months now, with Congress unwilling to go along with the President — until it voted for the Omnibus Budget Bill, which has the overtime changes tacked on and flapping loose, related to nothing in particular. Once again, what Congress rejected when it was last asked will now become the law of the land.

Then there's meat labeling. Overcoming the power of the meat industry lobby, Congress managed to pass a law requiring labels that show what country their products come from. The industry complained that they needed another two-year delay to get ready. Congress said no, we've waited long enough. When the President signs the Omnibus Budget Bill, guess what industry gets its two-year delay?

For purposes of this conversation, my own opinion on these four issues doesn't matter. What matters is that *we're about to live under new laws that were **just rejected** weeks or even days ago when they were considered on their own.* We have to wake up from our accumulated cynicism about the workings of Washington and understand how deeply twisted — how, for those of us who still believe in this country, deeply *unAmerican* — this is.

And do you know what? If you said that to members of Congress who have just voted for the Omnibus Bill, I don't think you'd get much argument. They might say that you're exaggerating, that "there's no need to get so worked up," but they wouldn't defend this as a responsible way to do business. What they will say instead is they had no choice — that the squabbling had gone on too long already, that there was no responsible solution in sight, that at some point they just had to hold their noses and fund the operations of the federal government before anyone was seriously hurt. "It's too bad, but *we HAD to do it.*"

Now let's be very clear exactly what members of Congress or the President are saying when they say that. They are saying that the sponsors of this bill took hostages that had to be saved. They took hostage food and welfare aid to the most vulnerable Americans. They took hostage Social Security payments to defenseless seniors. They took gravely ill Medicare recipients hostage. All these programs and more were lined up with guns pointed at their heads, and we couldn't let them die.

This, ladies and gentlemen, is legislative terrorism. Approval of this bill in its final form is giving in to terrorists, a practice that most of those who voted for this bill would normally pound the table to denounce. They would say when you give in to terrorism you only encourage more terrorism down the road. And they're right. With the passage of this bill, I don't even want to think about the rejects and rip-offs that will find their places in next year's omnibus spending bill.

What *I* say is: no, Representative, no, Senator, you did not have to pass this bill. No, Mr. President, you do not have to sign it. What you can do instead — what *will* be done instead, if I'm President the next time we see a replay of this sorry drama — is to strip the bill of all the garbage that couldn't pass on its own merits and introduce a clean and honest budget bill.

And I won't listen to all the worried clucking about the human damage that this delay will cause. You call out for pizza, hand the bill back to the Congressional staff who put it together, tell them to pull out all the eleventh-hour clunkers they stuffed into it, lock the doors, and have a clean straightforward bill back on the House floor for a vote within 24 hours. Anyone who tells you that can't be done isn't interested in doing the people's business in an honest, accountable way, period.

We have to stand up. We have to say that we won't deal with legislative terrorists, and we have to show that we mean it. The toxic cynicism that this business-as-usual breeds will bring America down unless we enforce a premise that we all learned as kids, the very first time we learned about our Constitution: the laws of this land will be those passed on their merits by the Congress of the United States and signed by the President. I hope you'll tell your legislators loud and clear what we all know is true: their current excuse — "It may not be right, but we had to do it" — isn't good enough for America any more.

Thank you.

★ ★ ★ ★ ★

The discussion guide for this speech is on page 143.

★ III ★

Afterwords

Where to From Here?

Practical Words:
The 30-Second CounterSpot
A Tactical Note to Candidates Who Are
Considering Speeches for Grownups

★ ★ ★ ★ ★

Encouraging Words:
The Hidden Agreement
Why We May Be Closer Than We Think

★ ★ ★ ★ ★

Last Words (for now):
What's Our Part in This?
The Next Step

★ ★ ★ ★ ★

"Ideals are like stars:
you will not succeed in
touching them with your hands,
but like the seafaring man
on the ocean desert of waters,
you choose them as your guides,
and following them,
you reach your destiny."

CARL SCHURZ
(1829–1906)

Practical Words

The 30-Second CounterSpot (2 Versions)

*A Tactical Note to Candidates Who Are
Considering Speeches for Grownups*

Are you a candidate? Then here's what you're thinking: *sound as any of these speeches are, I can't deliver them in the age of television. I'd get shredded.* You're imagining your opponents writhing with pleasure as they hear one of these speeches, just counting the ways they're going to shove your words back down your throat

They will try. In the political world we've created, nuanced explanations — the ones that acknowledge the strengths of opposing positions, that admit that benefits come with costs, that aren't hemmed in by sacred cows — are manna from heaven for a good campaign "communications" director. If, for example, you oppose the War on Drugs by giving the speech that I called "The Definition of Insanity" (Chapter IX), you'll be saying to a live audience

> "If you tell me we have to fight this battle without doing anything about the advertising-fueled multi-billion dollar trade in tobacco and hard alcohol, without challenging the massive overprescription of so-called medicines to increase the profits of politically powerful industries,

then I will tell you to count me out. I won't waste my time on hypocritical ventures that are sure to fail, and I hope you don't either..."

After you do, you can take it to the bank that you'll soon be watching a TV spot that goes something like this: an ominous off-screen voice, probably over grainy black-and-white footage of someone sticking a big needle in his arm, will say "When it comes to fighting to keep our kids safe from drugs, here's what" (your name goes here) "has to say." Then you'll see yourself at the podium, all earnest and serious, saying "I will tell you to count me out."

What to do? The same thing you'll be doing if you deliver any of these speeches: treat voters as if they were grownups. Tell them exactly what's going on. Yes, it's challenging in a 30-second spot (and yes, you do have to use TV to fight TV), but it can be done. Here's one way.

Grownups TV Spot #1

[relaxed environment, addressing camera directly, with a light, friendly "what are you gonna do with these guys?" tone]

HI, I'M _____

HERE'S ONE SAD THING ABOUT POLITICS: IF YOU TREAT AMERICANS LIKE GROWNUPS AND TALK HONESTLY ABOUT THE PROS AND CONS OF A SERIOUS ISSUE, YOU **KNOW** YOUR OPPONENTS WILL TAKE FROM YOUR SPEECH ONE TINY SNIPPET THAT SOUNDS STUPID BY ITSELF AND MAKE A TV

ATTACK AD OUT OF IT. SO IF YOU HEAR ME QUOT-
ED SAYING SOMETHING BRIEF AND ESPECIALLY
STUPID,

[insert graphic:

Get the whole story at
www.wholestory.org or 1-800-___-___
Then decide

leave on screen for the rest of the ad]

FIRST GET THE WHOLE STORY. THEN DECIDE FOR YOUR-
SELF WHO'S OFFERING COMMON-SENSE SOLUTIONS
AND WHO'S OFFERING TWISTED TV COMMERCIALS
AND PRAYING HARD THAT YOU WON'T NOTICE.

THANK YOU

Here's another:

Grownups TV Spot #2

HI, I'M _____

YOU MAY HAVE HEARD SOME REALLY ODD WORDS
COME OUT OF MY MOUTH IN MY OPPONENT'S TV
COMMERCIALS. MOST LIKELY I REALLY SAID THEM.

THIS IS CALLED *GOTCHA* POLITICS: TAKE YOUR
OPPONENT'S SPEECH ON A TOUGH, CHALLENGING
ISSUE, CAREFULLY PULL OUT ONE SENTENCE THAT
BY ITSELF MIGHT ANGER OR OFFEND PEOPLE, PUT IT

IN THE MIDDLE OF A TV ATTACK AD, AND...
GOTCHA! **THIS IS EXACTLY** WHY MOST POLITICIANS
ARE AFRAID TO TALK TO YOU LIKE GROWNUPS
ABOUT OUR COMPLEX PROBLEMS.

[insert graphic:

Get the whole story at
www.wholestory.org or 1-800-___-____
Then decide

leave on screen for the rest of the ad]

I'M NOT. I AM POSITIVE YOU'RE READY FOR THE WHOLE
STORY INSTEAD OF FALLING FOR GOTCHA TRICKS. GO
TO WHOLESTORY.ORG ON THE WEB, OR WRITE
_____, AND MAKE UP YOUR OWN MIND. NO
MATTER HOW SOME PEOPLE TRY TO SLICE-AND-DICE
MY WORDS FOR SNEAKY TV ADS, I WILL ALWAYS TALK
TO YOU LIKE GROWNUPS.

Try it. They'll like it.

Encouraging Words

The Hidden Agreement

Why We May Be Closer Than We Think

[This commentary originally appeared in *Spirituality and Health* Magazine in 2002]

It was just a warm-up question. I was beginning an hour-long live interview with Rabbi Michael Lerner on my daily public radio talk show, *The Jefferson Exchange*. He'd been on the show about a year earlier, so I asked him if any special insights had come to him since then.

Michael's life is rich with insight. He is the founder and editor of *Tikkun* Magazine, Rabbi of a large vibrant congregation in San Francisco and author of *The Politics of Meaning* and *Spirit Matters*, both required reading for anyone serious about social transformation in contemporary America. Shortly after becoming First Lady, Hillary Clinton seized on *The Politics of Meaning* as a foundational text for the new Administration and the media began to call Michael the White House Guru. That lasted until some journalists actually read and started quoting from the book, moving the Clintons to say that actually, now that they thought about it, they weren't really that interested in Michael and his ideas after all.

"Well, in fact, yes," the Rabbi answered. "I have been talking with an awful lot of people since *Spirit Matters* came out. All kinds of different people, from different cultures, generations, ethnic and income groups, parts of the country, really a wide range. And I'm hearing the same two things from just about everyone I have a real conversation with. The same two things *everywhere*, from *everyone*."

Here he paused with a small smile. "The first one is that people want a society different from the one we have. They want a community, a nation, an economy, a world, based more on the values of community, generosity, compassion and love, and less on hierarchy, acquisition and win/lose competition. That's the first thing.

"The *second* thing is this: they think they're alone. They think that they're the only ones who feel that way. They look around them and they see no reflection or support for the values they want, so they decide they're just being unrealistic, and that they just have to get a grip and adjust to the world as it really is. And so the wheel turns. And so the world goes."

In the days and weeks that followed I heard myself repeating the Rabbi's words whenever anyone talked about changing public consciousness — or, less ambitiously, about nudging public opinion on a particular issue. Almost everyone hearing it would pause, and I imagined I could hear their thought process move from the concept to a question: *what if it's true?*

What if most Americans really do share a longing for values that connect and nurture people? What if everything we see to the contrary — the "He who dies with the most toys" vector that seems to drive economy and society, the staggering levels of individual consumption, the fear-filled arguments and political struggles that make up every day's news — what if it's all a thin layer of mental noise, a story that we accept as real just because, out of unthinking habit, we expect it to be? Could we be creating and projecting into the future, for no reason at all, a world that's colder, lonelier, grimmer and more hollow than the one anyone wants?

We could be. And if we are, then the task of shifting the nation and the world towards peace and sustainable abundance becomes a lot easier. It's not the immense (some would say impossible) task of changing the consciousness and values of hundreds of millions of people. Instead it's the task of shining light and drawing to the surface values they already have, some of which barely flicker beneath layers of cynicism and surrender.

That doesn't make the task easy. The mainstream cultural messages that lure us to consume and conform and that ridicule sacred, non-material thinking aren't there by accident. They won't quietly fade away the first time a few people shout that the Emperor has no clothes, because they effectively serve some dominant groups that do very well with the world as it is, thank you very much. But they're not omnipotent. Or rather they are only when most of us unconsciously decide, unbeknownst to each other, that an alternative world that values connection over consumption isn't possible.

When we come to look back on our lives, there's some chance that we'll have to come to terms with disappointment at how little we moved the world towards a higher possibility. It would be one thing, and at least a small comfort, if we could say, "We couldn't do much because our values and beliefs were just too different from the core values of the vast American majority. We just weren't born at the right time. Too bad, but that's the way it goes."

That's not a pleasant thought. But it would be easier to bear than another conclusion: that in terms of American's beliefs and values, we were born at just the right time, that we had all the human raw material for social transformation that we needed and didn't know what to do with it. We didn't even know we had it.

What a miserable outcome that would be. The chance to head it off is worth trying almost anything, including more and deeper communication with people who seem to think differently than we do. Agreed?

Last Words (for now)

What's Our Part in This?

The Next Step

Speeches like these could break the downward cycle of American politics. Candidates will start making them if they start believing we're grownups. What can you and I do to help them believe that?

We can act like grownups. That includes staying awake during the election-year lullabies, and staying engaged between elections to prove that the things that we say are important to us really are. It means acknowledging and thanking the people we elect when they serve the public interest and stubbornly holding them accountable when they don't, and knowing issues well enough to recognize the difference.

And it means not throwing a tantrum when their positions take into account long-term costs, and the need to represent different parts of their constituency — when, in other words, they don't give us everything we want. Tantrums often take the form of single-issue voting, which is the civic version of what we did one-to-eight decades ago when we said "If you don't do what I say I won't be your friend anymore."

You might say that some issues are so important that they *should* determine your vote. I think you're right. But how many? When your list grows longer than two or three items, political leaders aren't going to see or treat you as a grownup. There's no reason they should.

If we can do all of this, we'll start hearing the kinds of speeches you've just read. Then we'll start electing the kind of people that give them.

But how exactly do we get from here to there? What are effective *specific* steps we can take to convince political leaders that we're grownups?

We're going to figure that out together. Let's meet at

www.asifweweregrownups.org

and see what we come up with.

★ IV ★

Questioning Words

*A Discussion Guide for Students
(Official or Otherwise)
to Stimulate
Debate and Insight*

★ ★ ★ ★ ★

★ ★ ★ ★ ★

"Question with boldness even the existence of God; because, if there be one, He must more approve of the homage of reason, than that of blind-folded fear."

THOMAS JEFFERSON

One

You Should Pay for My Campaign

*Telling a National Shriners Meeting
It's Time for Public Campaign Financing*

DISCUSSION GUIDE:

1. What does the speaker single out as the most widely-shared political opinion in the country? Do you agree? Are there other political opinions that you think almost everyone shares?

2. How does the speaker reconcile a critique of big money in politics with the fact that s/he's a "serious," i.e., well-funded, candidate? Is it a reasonable point?

3. What are the shortcomings of past attempts at campaign finance reform?

4. Are you concerned that public financing would "force people to support candidates they don't like?" What's the speaker's view on that? Are there other arguments against public financing that seem stronger to you?

5. Why do some claim that Americans have overwhelmingly rejected public financing already?

6. Why does the speaker believe that public financing, which could trigger billions of tax dollars in new spending, would be a bargain?

7. What's the most compelling part of the speaker's argument? What's the weakest?

8. Could this speech change the opinion of someone who doesn't support public financing? Why or why not?

★ ★ ★ ★ ★

TWO

On the Contrary...

Telling the Automobile Association of America the Price of Gasoline is Too Low

DISCUSSION GUIDE:

1. What strategies are mentioned for bringing down the cost of gasoline? Are there others that might be effective?

2. What's the speaker's "practical touchstone" for making decisions? What's the reason for emphasizing it so much in this speech? Do you think it's an effective approach?

3. What's the speaker's attitude towards the Seventh Generation ideal? Why does he modify it to the Third Generation?

4. What's the visual image the speaker wants the audience to ponder? What's the purpose of emphasizing it? Is there another image that would have worked as well or better?

5. What's the speaker's evidence that dramatic transportation alternatives are possible?

6. What use does the speaker make of America's current military spending in this proposal?

7. The speaker describes one "cold reality" as a major challenge in the short run. What is it, and how hard would it be to overcome?

8. What are the five parts of the speaker's proposal to change transportation? Are there any others you would add?

9. What's the most compelling part of the speaker's argument? What's the weakest?

10. Could this speech change the opinion of someone who has been demanding lower gasoline prices? Why or why not?

★ ★ ★ ★ ★

Three

"No Amount is Too Much..."

Telling the Veterans of Foreign Wars
Military Spending is Too High

DISCUSSION GUIDE:

1. Would the opening of this speech tend to make the audience receptive to the ideas that follow? Why or why not?

2. Why is it difficult to determine the total amount of America's military spending?

3. What practice does the speaker single out as the most inconsistent with genuine conservatism? Can you think of an argument to support the practice?

4. Why does the speaker create analogies between military spending and spending in our private lives? Is it an effective technique here? Why or why not?

5. How does the speaker deal with the notion that less military spending will put many people out of work? Is it an effective response?

6. The speaker believes that anyone who supports a level of military spending that is greater than that of all the rest of the nations combined would have to start with a basic belief about how the world works. What is that basic belief? What is your opinion of it? Could a reasoning person support the current level of U.S. military spending *without* holding that belief?

7. What are the two parts of the speaker's argument that too much military spending makes America less secure? How persuasive is each part?

8. What's the most compelling part of the speaker's argument? What's the weakest?

9. Could this speech change the opinion of someone who has fully supported U.S. military spending up until now? Why or why not?

★ ★ ★ ★ ★

Four

To Secure the Blessings of Liberty

Telling the Christian Coalition of America
Gay Marriage Should Not Be Banned

DISCUSSION GUIDE:

1. Describe the position on this issue that the speaker calls "trying to thread a tiny needle." Do you agree that it seems more like a political maneuver than a genuine belief?

2. Do you believe that the issue of same-sex marriage should be decided at the state level? Why or why not? What is the strongest argument for the federal government to take on the issue?

3. Generally speaking what kinds of issues do you think are most appropriately addressed by the states, and what kinds by the federal government?

4. On a scale of one to ten, how likely do you think it is that the U.S. Constitution will be amended to ban gay marriage in the next ten years? Why?

5. What is the "bad trade" the speaker describes? Do you agree with this view? Why or why not?

6. What is the speaker's concept of the line at which individual personal liberties should be restricted? Would you draw the line at the same place or not?

7. Why does the speaker bring up the hypothetical notions of banning televangelists or Creation Theory?

8. What's the most compelling part of the speaker's argument? What's the weakest?

9. Could this speech change the opinion of someone who wants to ban same-sex marriage? Why or why not?

★ ★ ★ ★ ★

Five

What Does It Symbolize?

Telling the American Legion
Flag Burning Should Be Legal

DISCUSSION GUIDE:

1. Why does the speaker make a point of stressing that he or she has never been in combat? What effect do you think that admission would have on this audience?

2. What is the "double talk" that the speaker thinks some listeners might hear in this speech?

3. What does the speaker mean by "the quality of freedom that sets America apart from countless nations throughout history who have claimed to be free?"

4. What impact does the speaker believe that flag-burning has on the opinion of observers? What about the impact on children? Do you agree?

5. With actual flag-burning incidents so rare, why do you think this issue comes up as often as it does?

6. What's the most compelling part of the speaker's argument? What's the weakest?

7. Could this speech change the opinion of someone who believes that flag-burning should be banned? Why or why not?

★ ★ ★ ★ ★

Six

The Two Most Powerful Words in America

Telling the U.S. Chamber of Commerce
We Need a National Health Care System

DISCUSSION GUIDE:

1. Beyond the obvious importance of human health, what are the factors that make health care such a central social and economic issue?

2. Why does the speaker think the words "socialized medicine" are so powerful?

3. How persuasive is the use of statistics in this presentation? Could this part of the speech have been improved?

4. What does the speaker think about the assumption that government programs are wasteful and poorly run? What do you think?

5. How does the speaker defend the claim that American health care is inadequate in light of the fact that people come from all over the world to be treated in the United States?

6. What is "single-payer" insurance as described here? Why does the speaker believe it would dramatically reduce costs?

7. According to the speaker what three additional characteristics are necessary for a high-quality health care system? How would you rank the three in importance? Are there other necessary factors the speaker hasn't mentioned?

8. What's the most compelling part of the speaker's argument? What's the weakest?

9. Could this speech change the opinion of someone who opposes a strong direct role for government in providing health care? Why or why not?

★ ★ ★ ★ ★

Seven

Stripping the Nation for Parts

*Telling the Iowa Farm Council
Government Shouldn't Subsidize Ethanol*

DISCUSSION GUIDE:

1. According to the speaker's logic, why is the issue of ethanol particularly important to presidential politics?

2. Why doesn't the speaker believe that ethanol is a smart investment? What does the speaker say could change his/her position?

3. What are top priorities of the speaker's energy policy? Why?

4. "What's the harm?" asks the speaker, in spending a tiny percentage of the federal budget on an ethanol program that may not be cost-effective. What is the harm?

5. In what way does the speaker call on Iowans to show America real leadership?

6. What's the most compelling part of the speaker's argument? What's the weakest?

7. Could this speech change the opinion of someone who wants the government to subsidize ethanol production? Why or why not?

★ ★ ★ ★ ★

Eight

The Camel's Damned Nose

Telling the National Abortion Rights Action League
to Compromise with its Opponents

DISCUSSION GUIDE:

1. Why does the speaker believe that it's especially hard for supporters of abortion rights to talk calmly about their disagreements? Do you agree?

2. What is the "practical reason" the speaker puts forward for considering compromise with those who oppose abortion rights? What do you think of this reasoning?

3. According to the speaker, why does the argument over abortion reach an absolute impasse?

4. What does the speaker believe to be the primary reason for strong opposition to restrictions like parental notification and 24-hour periods? Do you agree?

5. What does the speaker mean generally by the "camel's nose?" Do you agree that it's a significant problem?

6. Can you think of any approach or idea that could bring abortion rights supporters and foes together for worthwhile discussions?

7. What's the most compelling part of the speaker's argument? What's the weakest?

8. Could this speech change the opinion of an abortion rights supporter who opposes all compromise with opponents? Why or why not?

★ ★ ★ ★ ★

Nine

The Definition of Insanity, Illustrated

Telling the Anti-Drug Coalition of America
to Move Towards Legalization

DISCUSSION GUIDE:

1. How effective is the speaker's use of statistics? Is it about the right amount for a speech? Is there anything important that is missing? Would you have left anything out?

2. Why will the "charge up the hill" continue?

3. According to the speaker, what's the first concern of politicians when they talk about illegal drugs? Do you agree?

4. In the speaker's view, what makes adult warnings to their kids about illegal drugs so ineffective? Do you agree?

5. What does the speaker cite as proof that the U.S. can have more effective drug policies than it does?

6. Can you think of any important elements to the issue that aren't addressed here?

7. What's the most compelling part of the speaker's argument? What's the weakest?

8. Could this speech change the opinion of someone who strongly opposes relaxation of the laws and penalties against drugs? Why or why not?

★ ★ ★ ★ ★

Ten

Just Say NO to Legislative Terrorism

Telling the National Press Club
Why Must-Pass Budget Bills Must Be Vetoed

DISCUSSION GUIDE:

1. The speaker is urging the rejection of a bill that's needed to ease the suffering of some very vulnerable citizens. Why?

2. What important aspect of federal budget-making has dramatically changed over the years?

3. How has this change magnified the problem of "pork-barrel" spending, and opened the way to passage of measures that were recently rejected?

4. The speaker says that wasteful federal spending has three major practical consequences. What are they? Is this an effective way to frame the argument against "pork?"

5. What is the main point of the story the speaker tells about producing a television documentary?

6. What part of the process does the speaker call "deeply unAmerican?" Do you agree?

7. Is the speaker justified in calling this process "terrorism?" Why or why not?

8. What's the most compelling part of the speaker's argument? What's the weakest?

9. Could this speech change the opinion of someone who believes that legislation like this is too urgent to veto? Why or why not?

Acknowledgements

★ ★ ★ ★ ★

More people than I can remember have lent this project their skill, energy and faith. In the loaned skill category, I have to start with Terrie Claflin, my periodic breakfast pal, who knew the right questions and just when to ask them. She also took precious time that she should have been spending on her own book to give this manuscript a needed once-over with red ink. Now get cracking, Terrie, because there are some lovely Harley tales we've been waiting patiently to read.

A key moment as this project took shape was the instant reaction of Les AuCoin, a fine Congressman and subsequently a fine and loyal friend. He listened for about 45 seconds before a big embracing smile spread across his face, a smile that told me — as he told me explicitly time and again in the weeks that followed — this project deserved my very best shot. That was high-value affirmation, because Les, as you may have noticed back in the introduction, knows this habitat well.

There are two other professional elements that infused this project with quality and class: the generously-shared publishing savvy of Steve Scholl at Riverwood Books and the graphic mastery of David Ruppe (the least temperamental artist I've ever worked with) at Impact Publications.

Other friends who stepped up with an inspired thought or enthusiasm at exactly the right time were Robb Moss, Mort Mondale, Paul Clark, Jim Fritz, Joanna Gabriel, John Fisher-Smith, Joanie McGowan, Steve Sendar, Nancy Lessard, Ruth Walsh of the League of Women Voters, Jon Lange, Dennis Mead-Shikaly, Paul Moss and KC Golden, the world's finest wee-bro.

Professor William Hughes of Southern Oregon University and AP Government teacher Bill Gabriel, the man who has made hundreds of smart Ashland High School students groan for a year and thank him for a lifetime, generated more momentum for the project by expanding its possibilities. They recognized the importance this book would make in their classrooms for the coming generation of citizens.

A few people dropped the ten dozen things they are doing to help bring this project to the attention of prospective publishers: Neale Donald Walsch, the New Thought world's Energizer Bunny, and Donna Corso, whose labors free him to hop where he wants; Cathy Shaw, the woman who wins political campaigns no one else can; and Jean Houston, who is doing more work of consequence with more grace in more parts of the world than even her fans appreciate.

Even with all this support there was doubt along the way. Have you ever sent out into the world a political or philosophical premise, perhaps an excited letter-to-the-editor, that seemed so incisive to you, that unlocked a critical door, that absolutely *nailed* what had to be said, without stirring any noticeable reaction? Then you know the doubt. Five people blasted that doubt to bits. Four were my steady partners in mischief and social invention, the increasingly notorious Relentless Optimists: Bill Kauth, Tej Steiner, Craig Comstock — thanks, Craig, for early editorial nudges — and Ron Kurtz.

The fifth is the woman who's graced my life in ways big and small. She carefully examined the manuscript for clarity. More importantly, she said "You *can't* not do this book" whenever I was thinking otherwise. "We need it too much. You can't even slow down, because we need it *now*." *Grownups* would not be in your hands right now without Molly McBeth. Thank you, Molly Jo.

★ ★ ★ ★ ★

Photo by Nancy Lessard

Jeff Golden has woven together his work in state, local and national politics, mediation and public broadcasting for twenty-five years. He is the founding president of the Oregon Guides Association, a former Jackson County, Oregon Commissioner, Oregon's first nominee for the John F. Kennedy Profile in Courage award, and the author of *Forest Blood* (www.forestblood.com), the pre-eminent novel of the Northwest timber wars.

Jeff spends far too much time on concrete. He lives in Ashland, Oregon, where his provocatively independent public radio talk show, *The Jefferson Exchange* (www.jeffexchange.org), originates every weekday. He spends time there with his children, Daniel and Sarah, in between their globe-trotting adventures.

We hope you decide to bring
more people to this conversation.

★ ★ ★ ★ ★

Visit **www.asifweweregrownups.org**
to place orders and find out about special discount prices
for college and university classes or
other discussion groups.

Or look for *As If We Were Grownups* at
your favorite bookstore.